BIRDS Of The
CANADIAN ROCKIES

BIRDS Of The CANADIAN ROCKIES

George W. Scotter
Tom J. Ulrich
Edgar T. Jones

Western Producer Prairie Books
Saskatoon, Saskatchewan

Western Producer Prairie Books
Saskatoon, Saskatchewan

The publisher wishes to acknowledge the support received for this publication from the Canada Council.

Printed and bound in Canada
8 7 6 5 4 3 2 1   97 96 95 94 93 92 91 90

Western Producer Prairie Books is a unique publishing venture located in the middle of western Canada and owned by a group of prairie farmers who are members of Saskatchewan Wheat Pool. From the first book in 1954, a reprint of a serial originally carried in the weekly newspaper, *The Western Producer,* to the book before you now, the tradition of providing enjoyable and informative reading for all Canadians is continued.

Canadian Cataloguing in Publication Data

Scotter, G. W. (George Wilby)

Birds of the Canadian Rockies

Includes bibliographical references.
ISBN 0-88833-305-6

1. Birds — Rocky Mountains, Canadian (B.C. and Alta.)
— Identification. I. Ulrich, Tom J. II. Jones, Edgar T. III. Title.

QL685.5.R63S36 1990   598.29711   C90-097026-X

Dedicated to the birds of the Canadian Rockies
May they always be present
to inspire all lovers of the beautiful

Figure 1. The southern portion of the Canadian Rocky Mountains and nearby areas.

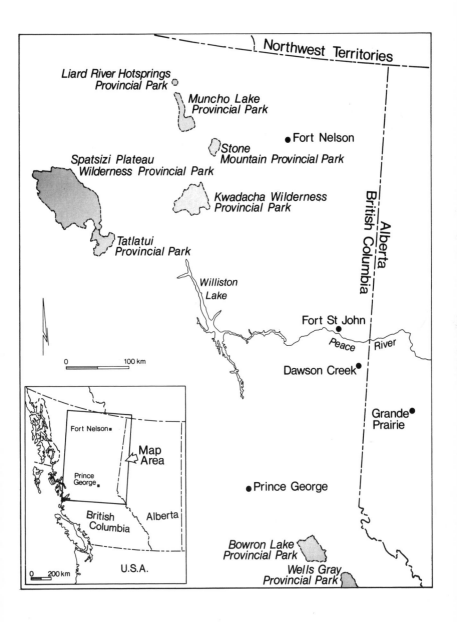

Figure 2. The northern portion of the Canadian Rocky Mountains and nearby areas.

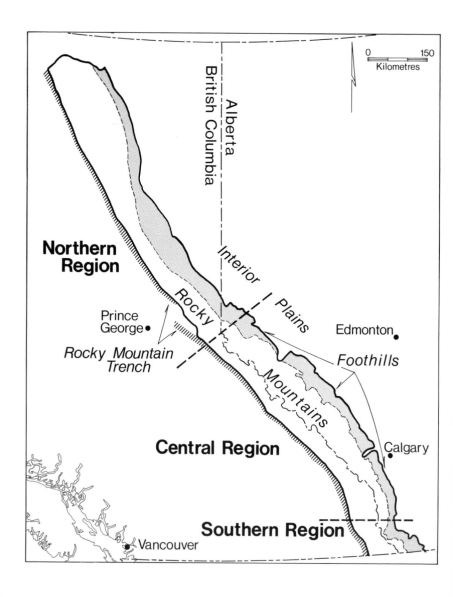

Figure 3. Regions in and near the Canadian Rocky Mountains.

Contents

Acknowledgments

We owe a debt of gratitude to a number of colleagues and friends who contributed to this book. Parts of the manuscript were read and many useful suggestions were made by Dave Elphinstone, Etta Scotter, Kevin Van Tighem, and Terry Thormin. Jerry Beyersbergen, Kenneth Fink, Bert Gildart, Gary Jones (courtesy of Edgar Jones), Danny On (courtesy of Glacier National Park), Alan Nelson, Robert Stevens, and Jan Wassink loaned photographs for inclusion in this book. Regional checklists of birds were updated by Wayne Campbell (northern British Columbia), Ron Chamney (Kananaskis Country), Heather Dempsey (Banff National Park), Larry Halverson (Kootenay National Park), Kevin Van Tighem (Jasper and Yoho national parks), Rob Watt (Waterton Lakes National Park), and Cleve Wershler (several areas in Alberta). Special appreciation goes to Shirley MacDougall and SMP Graphics for typing the manuscript and preparing the illustrations, respectively.

Introduction

Rapidly growing in popularity, bird watching now has an estimated thirty million participants in North America. Included among its devotees are people of all ages and walks of life. This book supplies residents and visitors in the Canadian Rockies with what they need to know to start an absorbing hobby that can last a lifetime and springboard them into deeper studies.

The purpose of *Birds of the Canadian Rockies* is to help anyone identify the birds he or she is most likely to see and to find particular bird species of interest. We hope this book will foster a greater interest in birds; that it will help users to know them better and to develop a much wider appreciation of nature, as well as a deeper understanding of the environment we share with these wild creatures within this striking segment of the Canadian landscape.

The Canadian Rocky Mountains (Figures 1 and 2) are the northern segment of a large mountain system widely known for its rugged vistas. In Canada, the Rockies extend nearly 1400 km from the American border at the 49th parallel to the Liard River, flanked on the west by the Rocky Mountain Trench and on the east by the Interior Plains (Figure 3).

The Canadian Rockies are aligned northwest-southeast, and divisible into ranges. The foothills, 25 to 50 km wide, rise above the Interior Plains as linear ridges and hills of Mesozoic shale and sandstone. The Rocky Mountain Trench marks a major fault line that is very distinct on satellite photos. The Muskwa Ranges of the northern Rocky Mountains are broadest and highest around Mount Sylvia (2942 m in elevation) near Kwadacha Wilderness Provincial Park. In that area, the terrain is as rugged as any other part of the Rockies, having been carved by glaciation from great sections of stratified rock. A number of glaciers continue to quarry the highest peaks.

The Rockies are narrow where crossed by the Peace River. To the south the Hart Ranges rise gradually and form a relatively subdued terrain, with summits under 2750 m in elevation. The Continental Ranges are linear, with great cliffs and precipitous faces of bare gray rock sculptured by glaciation from thick sections of limestone and dolomite. They are broad, and their summit elevations increase to that of the highest peak, Mount Robson (3954 m), west of Jasper in Mount Robson Provincial Park. A number of high peaks on the Continental Divide cluster around the Columbia Icefield, the largest of many glaciers in the Rockies. Southward, peaks up to 3600 m in elevation occur at intervals or in groups along the mountain backbone through the Lake Louise and Banff areas to Crowsnest Pass, south of which they are generally lower. Gadd (1986) provides an excellent outline of the geology and geography for the interested reader.

At first glance the trees and forests of the Canadian Rocky Mountains look like a continuous green carpet rolling up the mountainsides. Upon closer inspection three major vegetation zones, each with its own characteristic plants and animals, reveal themselves.

These zones form bands across the mountainsides—somewhat like the layers of a wedding cake. The bottom band, called the montane zone, is found in the valley bottoms. The subalpine zone forms the middle layer. The upper band, the alpine zone, is the land above the trees. One zone merges into another and there is much overlapping because of different topography, exposure, moisture, soil, and prevailing winds. Timberline is at about 2400 m in the south, 2100 m at Jasper, and 1500 m in the north. Several habitat and habitat complexes are found within these major vegetation zones, each with its characteristic birds. Habitats within the Canadian Rockies are unusually variable, ranging from rich riparian areas to glacier-covered alpine slopes.

Within the Canadian Rockies thousands of hectares of excellent bird habitat are preserved and protected in areas such as Glacier-Waterton International Peace Park, four national parks, many provincial parks, a few wilderness areas such as White Goat and Willmore, and wildlife refuges such as Wilmer, north of Invermere.

Of the more than 800 birds in North America, about 315 occur in the Canadian Rockies. This book provides information on identification, status, distribution, and habitat for more than 200 of these species. Many of the others are accidental, vagrants, or so rare that they are not likely to be encountered.

This book is arranged so that the text and the colored photographs face each other for speedy reference. The order in which the species appear in the text and their common and scientific names follow the American Ornithologists' Union Check-list (1983, 1985). This sequence is used by professional ornithologists and indicates the relationships among the birds. Following the common name is the approximate length, in centimeters, of each bird, representing a measurement taken from the tip of the bill to the tip of the tail as they would normally be seen in field situations. The scientific name follows below.

All known living plants and animals are arranged into a graded system based on physical resemblances. Every living thing belongs to a kingdom (plant or animal), a phylum, a class, an order, a family, a genus, and a species. The genus and species titles make up the formal name. These two-parted names are comparable to the way we give names to people belonging to different families. In scientific names, however, the first part tells the genus (group) to which the bird belongs; for example, *Gavia* means it is a loon. This is the same as a surname or family name, such as Jones. The second part of the name indicates the species (particular member of the group); for example, *immer,* which means "gray or blackened ashes of a fire," apparently refers to the plumage of the bird. This is comparable to the given name of an individual, such as Tom in Tom Jones. No two species share the same two-part scientific name. Ornithologists, unlike botanists and mammalogists, have agreed on standard common names, which greatly reduces confusion. Current common names are used throughout the text, with an occasional reference to local and older names included in some cases.

For all of the species described and illustrated we have added observations about their distribution within the Canadian Rocky Mountains. For convenience, the Rockies are divided into three major regions: northern, central, and southern. The northern region includes the Rockies north of Jasper National Park, the central region from Highway 3 to the northern boundary of Jasper National Park, and the southern region from the international boundary to Highway 3 (Figure 3).

The distribution of birds is generally well known in the southern and central regions but very little information is available for the north. Detailed studies of bird abundance and distribution at Waterton (Sharp, 1972), Yoho (Wade, 1977), Banff and Jasper (Holroyd and Van Tighem, 1983; Van Tighem and LeMessurier, 1988), and Kootenay (Poll *et al.*, 1984) were consulted, along with personal experience, in making those assignments. The only area in the northern region with detailed records is Liard Hotsprings. That site is technically beyond, but very near, the northern boundary of the Canadian Rockies. For that reason we have given distributions for Banff (B), Jasper (J), Kananaskis Country (KC), Kootenay (K), Liard River Hotsprings area (L), Waterton Lakes (W), and Yoho (Y). Distributions of other regions can be judged by their proximity to these areas. The Canadian Rockies are often referred to as simply "the Rockies" or "our area."

Certain terms are used for the status and abundance of birds within the Canadian Rockies. A bird that lives there all-year-round is called a resident, whereas a summer resident lives there only in the spring and summer, and a winter resident only during the winter. A migrant is a bird that travels through the region either casually or on its annual migrations. Terms such as common, uncommon, scarce, and rare when applied to abundance are subjective. No numerical values are implied. They are used as follows:

Common—a species that is likely to be seen daily in appropriate habitat during the appropriate season.

Uncommon—a species that an observer spending three days in the appropriate habitat and during the appropriate season can expect to see at least once but probably not daily.

Scarce or Occasional—a species that an observer spending a week in the appropriate habitat and during the appropriate season can expect to see at least once.

Rare—a species that occurs in such low numbers that it is unlikely to be seen on a week-long visit and would usually be observed only a few times a year.

The breeding status is given for those birds where an active nest or nests with eggs or offspring or of an adult bird with flightless young have been recorded. Territorial behavior or flying young were not considered as evidence of breeding. The lack of a breeding record for a species could indicate that it does not breed in the Canadian Rockies or that breeding has not yet been recorded.

Obvious distinctive features, which will aid in identifying each species, are given in the descriptions. Comparisons with similar species are made so that a user may watch for those characteristics that most readily distinguish one from the other. Plumage descriptions are generally limited to those of breeding adults. Field marks are the points to look for to distinguish quickly and accurately each species from others that closely resemble it. Special field markings such as wing and tail bars, rump patches, breast bands, bill shapes, head patterns, and eye-rings are included in the descriptions.

Many other factors are useful in identifying birds. In conjunction with field marks, learning a bird's voice, habits, and habitat can be very helpful. Also knowing where and when individual species normally occur and their status in selected areas of the Canadian Rockies is important.

Since the process of locating a particular bird is greatly simplified by knowing where to look, we have provided comments on the habitat preferences for each bird described. Most species of birds are limited to a specific habitat by adaptations that they have made to the physical and biological conditions found within that habitat or habitat complex. Birds that may be difficult to identify by appearance alone can often be placed by knowledge of typical habitats.

Birds, however, are not evenly distributed across their ranges. Some species are highly local and found nesting only in very specialized habitats. Black swifts, for example, nest on the walls of steep canyons, often near water. On the other hand, bank swallows require steep, sandy or gravelly banks for nesting.

Of course, birds have great mobility and most of them can tolerate a variety of habitats, especially during migration. Birds can be seen everywhere within the Canadian Rockies, so one should not be surprised to find a bird entirely out of its normal habitat.

Every bird will not be found on any given day at any given habitat. Bird watching is full of temporary disappointments and surprises. But it is always a challenge to find and identify birds and other wildlife in their natural environment.

Voice descriptions are included where we feel they aid identification. The vocalizations of birds may be divided into songs and calls. Songs are usually given by adult males on territory during the breeding season. Calls are generally more simple and are often given throughout the year by both sexes. Written descriptions of a bird's voice, while helpful, often vary among those describing the voice and may be difficult to interpret. We encourage readers to learn voices through actual field study and by listening to recordings (Kellogg, 1975). Once learned, most birds can be readily identified by voice alone. For some species, such as the flycatchers, knowing the voice is essential for positive identification. Songs can be distinguished according to pitch, cadence, duration, loudness, frequency of utterance, and quality. Knowing bird sounds vastly increases the efficiency and enjoyment of birders.

While our goal has been to keep technical terminology to an absolute minimum there is a need for readers to understand the basic structure and plumage of a bird. A glossary and diagram (Figure 4) of bird parts are included to assist the reader.

For identification we encourage the reader to use the photographs along with the text on the facing page. For most birds the photographs will illustrate the basic features and we have added information in the text important in identification. Most of the full-color photographs in this book are of adult males during the breeding season, since they are generally the most colorful and conspicuous and thus the easiest to identify. The females are usually a duller, much less colorful version. Most of the photographs are of birds in a characteristic pose in a natural setting, as they would normally be viewed at close range. Photographs closely resemble the way the human eye sees a bird so they add a dimension of realism and natural beauty. We also realize the limitations of the photographic approach. For this reason the reader may want to use this book in conjunction with one of the excellent field guides listed in the selected references.

For the user whose interest in birds is more than casual, a checklist of all species found in the Canadian Rockies is appended. This list is accurate to the date of completion of the manuscript (September 1989).

If you are a beginning bird watcher, the following may help improve your observations. Birds tend to avoid noise and commotion. You will see many more birds if you and your companions walk quietly and speak softly. Remember that various types of birds are active during different times. Songbirds are easiest to see after dawn, when they feed most briskly. The hour before sunset can be rewarding, also. During the rest of the day, many small birds are relatively sluggish and silent. Most water birds are easy to find throughout the day. Hawks and eagles hunt when visibility is best and when they can soar on the thermals. Most owls are active at night.

Also, beginners are encouraged to become familiar with family characteristics as this can save a great deal of time when identifying birds in the field. Keep in mind that the majority of bird species show variations in their plumages, which are correlated with age, sex, season, color phases, or geography. Some gulls, for example, may have a sequence of different plumages until they attain adulthood. The ability to identify birds accurately and efficiently in the field improves with practice and experience.

We believe that the color photographs, non-technical descriptions, and convenient size will make this book useful to the backpacker, mountain climber, highway traveler, kitchen-window birder, and generally curious-minded. We will have succeeded if we can introduce you to some of the treasures and gems waiting to be discovered in our Rocky Mountain inheritance. Being able to recognize the birds you encounter and to call them by name is an indispensable and exciting first step toward a deeper understanding and appreciation of the natural world around us.

Common Loon (60 cm)

BJKCKLWY*

Gavia immer

LOON FAMILY

Of the four species of loons that occur in the Canadian Rockies, only the common loon breeds there. It is commonly found alone or in pairs on montane and lower subalpine lakes. Mature birds sport a formal black-and-white appearance and are about the size of a goose. In the spring and summer both sexes have glossy black heads and necks with a finely checkered black-and-white back. Their lower throats have obvious necklaces of white, with narrow black lines that are narrow at the front of the neck and widen toward the back. The birds have startling red eyes and a 7-cm long, black bill that is straight and quite stout. These birds are well known for their wild wailings and their extraordinary ability to dive and swim beneath the water for 50 to 100 m before surfacing. Their song is one or more prolonged *"whoo-EEE-ooo"*'s followed by an insane laugh, which has given rise to the expression "looney" or "crazy as a loon." Nests are generally constructed at the water's edge so the nesting loon can reach the water quickly when threatened.

Pied-billed Grebe (23 cm)

BJKCKLW

Podilymbus podiceps

GREBE FAMILY

When disturbed, the pied-billed grebe has a remarkable ability to disappear almost instantly under water, apparently never to reappear. That mysterious elusiveness has caused it to be called such descriptive names as "helldiver" and "waterwitch." When an intruder is discovered, this grebe, by compressing its feathers and changing its specific gravity, can sink low in the water until on occasion only its bill projects above the surface. This rather odd-looking grebe has a large head and brown eyes. The short, thick, blunt beak is bluish white with a black band near the tip. This bird nests on lakes and ponds with considerable reeds and cattails in the montane zone. Floating nests are constructed of matted, aquatic vegetation. The four to seven young are precocial and are often seen riding on their parents' backs, even when the adults dive to feed. Despite the pied-billed's secretive nature, it has a loud and far-reaching voice which under favorable conditions can be heard for a kilometer or more.

Horned Grebe (25 cm)

BJKCKLWY

Podiceps auritus

GREBE FAMILY

The horned grebe is about the same size as the eared and pied-billed grebes. Horned and eared grebes have sharp, slender bills instead of thick, blunt bills like the pied-billed. The horned grebe has a rich chestnut neck and flanks. Its golden ear tufts, or "horns," glow against the jet black head. This grebe is distinguished from the eared by its red instead of black neck, its full ruff, and golden ear tufts that run from the eye to the upper back of the head instead of golden cheek plumes. In contrast to the eared and pied-billed grebes, the horned grebe often nests on lakes or ponds with bare shores and little cover. In full nuptial plumage these handsome little grebes perform a courtship dance in unison. They erect their tufts and ruffs, lift the body erect, and patter along the water on rapidly moving feet.

---

*Indicates distribution. See Introduction for explanation of letters.

Common Loon

Pied-billed Grebe

Horned Grebe

3

Red-necked Grebe (30 cm)
Podiceps grisegena

BJKCKLWY

GREBE FAMILY

Marked with a jet black crown, silvery white cheek patches, and a rich chestnut red neck, the red-necked grebe is easy to identify, even at long range. Its back is a mottled brown, the bill sharp and yellow, and the eyes red. Courtship rituals include the presenting of bits of nesting material to each other. They generally build a floating nest that is attached to surrounding vegetation. After incubation, the downy young, although excellent swimmers and divers, often climb on the back of the parents for a rest or a ride. These birds, like the loons, cannot get airborne from land, but must take off from water. Their loud, raucous calls add to the interest of any marsh. Red-necked grebes are fairly common breeding birds in the central and northern parts of the Canadian Rockies; they are less abundant in the south.

Eared Grebe (23 cm)
Podiceps nigricollis

BJKCKLWY

GREBE FAMILY

Eared grebes are gregarious birds that often form loose colonies in large, reed-bordered, shallow sloughs or lakes. Their floating nests, fragile in construction and on water only 20 to 30 cm deep, may be so closely spaced that a canoe can hardly pass between them without causing damage. The smallest of the grebes in our area, the eared has a black neck and a spray of golden plumes on the cheek fanning out behind the red eye and a dark, helmetlike crest on the crown. The birds seldom leave the nesting site from spring arrival until their fall departure. This grebe feeds mostly at or near the water surface, a trait distinctive from the other grebes in this locale. There are no nesting records for the eared grebe in our area.

Western Grebe (46 cm)
Aechmophorus occidentalis

BJKCKLWY

GREBE FAMILY

A superb swimmer and diver, the western grebe is one of the largest grebes in North America. It has a long, swanlike neck and is black on its upperparts and white below. The black crown extends below the red eyes and lores in contrast with Clark's grebe, which is extremely similar except that its black crown does not extend to the eyes or the lores. The greenish yellow bill is slender, sharp, and slightly uptilted. Some of the courtship displays of these birds are spectacular. Early in the courtship, bits of nest material are passed from bill to bill to establish pair bonding. Later, the pair rear up vertically with heads held horizontally and necks kinked and spring side-by-side over the water's surface on rapidly moving feet. Such rituals culminate with a plunge below the surface. Nesting generally occurs in colonies on large lakes edged with reeds. As with other grebes, the young often ride piggyback on the parents' backs, partly hidden by the wing coverts. Western grebes are spring and fall migrants within the Canadian Rockies.

Red-necked Grebe

Eared Grebe

Western Grebe

American White Pelican (127 cm)   BJW
Pelecanus erythrorhynchos   PELICAN FAMILY

Despite their huge size, pelicans with their slow wingbeat are efficient fliers and often soar at great heights where they delight in acrobatics. It is a beautiful sight to see these white birds with black wing tips fly, evenly spaced in long lines, shimmering in the sunshine and contrasted against a deep blue lake or azure sky. Breeding birds are the most conspicuous with a pale yellow crest and a fibrous plate on the bright orange, upper mandible. The pelican, with an enlarged bill and a large bill pouch, is a fishing specialist. The pouch, approximately 45 cm long and 15 cm deep and capable of holding several liters, is employed in scooping up fish and other small, aquatic animals. After a catch, they squeeze their bill against their throat forcing water out the sides of the beak, then swallow the food. Pelicans are communalistic and nest in colonies on islands or other isolated spots on large lakes, with the parents sharing the responsibilities of rearing the young. Young birds feed on regurgitated "soup" from the pouches of their parents. Later in life they reach into the parent's gullet for predigested meals. They are present in the Canadian Rockies only during spring and autumn migrations.

American Bittern (58 cm)   BJKCWY
Botaurus lentiginosus   HERON FAMILY

American bitterns are bog and marsh haunters, much preferring a thick cover of grasses and reeds to open water. Their long neck, set off by black streaks, dangling legs, and rich yellowish brown upperparts make these birds easy to recognize. When disturbed the American bittern, with its camouflage coloration, freezes motionless among the marsh plants with the neck extended and beak pointed skyward; only a keen observer will detect its location. During the spring, however, its bizarre song betrays its presence. The distinctive *"pump-er-lunk"* song, repeated several times, has been compared to the noise made by an old, wooden water pump. Once learned, the remarkable call is unmistakable. The javelin-like bill is used to snap up a variety of water creatures. Their platform nests are generally well hidden in the marsh vegetation. American bitterns are occasionally seen in the Canadian Rockies and there are nesting records from Banff.

American White Pelican

American White Pelican with young

American Bittern

Great Blue Heron (100 cm)

Ardea herodias

BJKCKLWY

HERON FAMILY

Our largest heron, the great blue, is a long-necked, long-legged wading bird standing a meter or more in height. Its head is white with broad black stripes on either side. The upperparts are mainly grayish blue; underparts are variously streaked with black and white. During the breeding season, the head, lower neck, and back are ornated with long, slender plumes. In flight the neck is folded into the shoulders, and the legs held stiffly behind the body. When feeding in a lake or slow-moving stream, the great blue heron stands with an alertly extended neck or in a hunched position. This bird will stand statuesquely until a meal swims or wanders into striking range, or it may cautiously wade with almost imperceptible movement. At any moment it may shoot out a large, sharply pointed bill with lightning speed to impale inattentive creatures. They dine on fish, frogs, snakes, large insects, and small rodents. Nests, generally built in the highest treetops, are established in rookeries of various sizes and the sites are used year after year.

Tundra Swan (90 cm)

Cygnus columbianus

BJKCKLWY

WATERFOWL FAMILY

Although these swans nest on the arctic tundra, they are frequently seen resting on lakes in the Canadian Rockies during both the spring and autumn migrations, staying for several days at a time. Tundra swans and trumpeter swans are similar in appearance. Both are large birds with all-white plumage, very long necks, and black legs and feet. The tundra, however, is smaller in size, lighter in weight, and has a shorter wingspan. Many, but not all tundra swans, have a small, yellow spot at the base of the bill, close to the eye. Trumpeter swans lack this marking. The most distinctive difference is the call. That of the tundra swan is rather like the Canada goose, but is higher pitched and more melodious. These birds were formerly called "whistling swans" because of the sound made by the powerful beating of their wings in flight, often mistaken for the voice of the birds.

Great Blue Heron

Tundra Swan

Tundra Swan

9

Trumpeter Swan (114 cm)
Cygnus buccinator

Largest of the world's swans, the trumpeter was once nearly extinct. Through management efforts the numbers of this graceful and picturesque bird are increasing. The only field characteristic that can be used for certain to separate the two native swans is the voice. The trumpeter swan has a low-pitched, brief *"beep"* call that is resonant, brassy, and trombonelike (compare with tundra swan). The white feathers of the head and upper neck often become stained an orange color as a result of feeding or grubbing activities in areas rich with iron. These elegant birds mate for life and may raise three to six cygnets a year. For several years, trumpeter swans have nested east and north of Waterton Lakes National Park and near Tumbler Ridge, British Columbia, within the Canadian Rockies.

Snow Goose (48 cm)
Chen caerulescens

Snow geese occur in two color variants, one white with black wing tips and the other blue-gray with a white neck and head. Both color phases frequently have their heads, necks, and upperparts rust-stained from feeding in iron-impregnated soil and water. The bill in both variants is rosy pink with the exception of a blackish arc called a "grinning patch" or "smile." This patch, found on both sides of the upper and lower mandibles, consists of serrated edges used for cutting plants for food. A northern breeder, the snow goose is seen in our area only during spring and autumn migrations. The noisiest of geese, the skeins of thousands of "snows" make the skies ring with their high-pitched *"kowk."* They often settle like fresh snow on golden stubble fields to graze on their favorite green grasses before continuing their journey.

Trumpeter Swan

Snow Goose

Snow Goose (blue phase)

Canada Goose (40 to 65 cm)
Branta canadensis

Among the sights and sounds of nature, one of the most beautiful is a gaggle of honking geese set majestically against the spring or autumn sky, announcing the passing of the season. The Canada goose is one of the best-known and most widely distributed birds in North America. Its distinctive V-shaped skeins and loud *"un HWONK"* are familiar to many people. Biologists speculate that the lead goose and each goose behind it in the familiar V-formation "breaks trail" making it easier for those behind to fly and save precious energy. This bird is gray-brown with a black head and neck, distinct white cheek patches, and a light-colored breast. The bill and legs are black. Size is quite variable, depending on which of ten races the goose belongs to. Some are scarcely larger than mallards, others are over four times that size. Known for their strong family loyalties, Canada geese usually mate for life; both parents share the responsibility of caring for the nest and young. The Canada goose is both a resident breeder and migrant in the Canadian Rockies. Small islands in lakes and rivers, muskrat houses, hawk nests, and cliffs in river valleys make ideal nesting sites. They readily take to man-made, open nestboxes, also.

Wood Duck (34 cm)
Aix sponsa

Considered by many as the most beautiful duck in North America, if not the world, the male wood duck in its multicolored red, brown, white, blue, and green breeding plumage is unexcelled. In addition to its iridescent plumage, red eye, and conspicuous red-and-white bill, the "woodie" has a long, flowing, down-hanging crest on the head, a relatively long rectangular tail, and distinctive white face markings. Although less showy, the female is also beautiful. At close range the white, teardrop-shaped eye-ring of the female is quite conspicuous, as are the light-colored throat and head crest. Wood ducks nest in hollow trees near water. They take readily to artificial nestboxes, also. Unlike the typical yellowish ducklings of dabbling ducks, the young of wood ducks are white below and dark above.

Canada Goose

Wood Duck (male)

Wood Duck (female)

13

Green-winged Teal (27 cm)

Anas crecca

Our smallest duck, the green-winged teal is known for its speed and aerobatic abilities during flight. The male is a delicately marked bird with a bold chestnut head and neck broken by an extensive patch of iridescent green extending from the eye down the side of the neck, neatly outlined by a narrow band of white. The female is nondescript, mottled and spotted in buffs and browns. They spend much of their time on shallow sloughs tipping for food. When not feeding, they enjoy sunning, often standing on one leg with the bill tucked under a wing. Green-wings breed in the Canadian Rockies and a brood usually numbers ten to twelve ducklings.

Mallard (40 cm)

Anas platyrhynchos

Among the earliest harbingers of the prairie spring, the mallard is the most abundant and widespread duck in North America. The mallard is the most common duck in the Rockies, sometimes on a year-round basis in the most favorable habitats. Mallards are known as "dabbling" or "puddle" ducks because they prefer to feed on or near the surface of shallow bodies of water. Breeding drakes are much more colorful than hens for most of the year. Males have a characteristic glossy green head, narrow white neck collar, chestnut brown breast, and grayish body. The rump and upcurved tail feathers are black. During the summer molt the drakes closely resemble the hens. Hens are straw brown, streaked with dark brown, and have a white tail. In both sexes, the undersides of the wings are flashing white when the bird is in flight, and the legs and feet are reddish orange. The bill is orange-splotched with black in the hens compared with yellow-green or drab olive in the drakes. The bright blue speculum is bordered with white on both edges for the drake and hen.

Northern Pintail (47 cm)

Anas acuta

Along with the first Canada geese and mallards, northern pintails return in the spring as soon as water is available in the prairie sloughs. Pintails are long, slender, graceful ducks. The drake in nuptial plumage is boldly but tastefully marked with muted shades of brown, gray, black, and white. Its chocolate-colored head and neck is broken by a white fingerlike stripe that extends from the white breast. His prominent, pointed, black tail feathers give the species its name. In eclipse plumage, the drakes closely resemble the mottled grayish brown hens, except for their bills. The hen has a dark, mainly grayish blue bill while that of the drake is bluish gray with a dark, longitudinal center stripe. Their speculum varies from metallic green to bronze-purple. It is preceded on the forewing by a band of chestnut and bordered behind by black and white. They are dabblers and, because of their long necks, are able to feed in deeper water than some other ducks, taking whatever food is locally abundant. Pintails are fairly common on lakes and marshes within the Canadian Rockies during migration.

J. WASSINK

Green-winged Teal (male)

T. ULRICH

Mallard (male and female)

T. ULRICH

Northern Pintail (male)

15

Blue-winged Teal (28 cm)

Anas discors

A small duck, the blue-winged teal drake is slightly larger than the hen. In full breeding plumage, the drakes are gray-brown, with large, white rump patches, a black tail, and a distinctive white crescent in front of each eye. In eclipse plumage the drake closely resembles the plain, mottled brown hen. In all plumages the bright blue forewing shoulder patches identify this attractive little duck. A narrow white border separates the blue area from an iridescent green speculum that is bordered by black on the other sides. Primarily a surface feeder, the "blue-wings" frequent the shallow edges close to shore. They fly in tight flocks, twisting and turning at breakneck speed just above the marsh vegetation. They wait until the spring is well advanced before journeying northward and they leave early in the autumn. During migration blue-winged teals are locally abundant in small flocks on lakes and rivers in our area.

Cinnamon Teal (29 cm)

Anas cyanoptera

Of the three species of teal in the Canadian Rockies, the cinnamon is the least common although its numbers seem to be increasing. They are known to breed from Banff southward in our area. Cinnamon teal are shallow-water ducks similar to other teal. The drake cinnamon teal is a uniformly rich cinnamon or chestnut color on the body and head and has a large, cerulean blue patch on the leading edge of the forewing. The speculum is iridescent green with black borders. Except for the blue wing patch the hen is rather nondescript. The females of all the teal species are difficult to tell apart in the field.

Northern Shoveler (35 cm)

Anas clypeata

Northern shovelers, or "spoonbills" as they are often called locally, are a mallard-look-alike except for the huge, black, spoon-shaped bill and smaller size. Breeding males have a green head and neck, white breast, and bright chestnut underparts that extend around the flanks. Like other surface-feeding ducks, the hen shoveler has a plumage pattern of buffs and browns. In addition to being a means of identifying the bird, the bill is a highly efficient feeding tool. It has a series of well-developed, comblike teeth or lamellae along the edges that act as filters. By movements of its bill through water and semiliquid mud, the shoveler takes in water and silt and strains out tiny food particles. The particles include insects and their larvae, crustaceans, and the seeds, leaves, and stems of plants. In addition, the northern shovelers upend and dive under water to obtain their food requirements. Northern shovelers are seen occasionally in the Canadian Rockies and probably breed only in the southern part.

Blue-winged Teal (male)

T. ULRICH

Cinnamon Teal (male and female)

T. ULRICH

Northern Shoveler (male)

E. JONES

17

Gadwall (37 cm)

BJKCWY

Anas strepera

Perhaps the least colorful of the ducks in our region, the gadwall has no bright colors, no eye-rings, and no flank flashes. Instead, plumage of the drake is an overall brown-gray pattern that is broken by a black rear end and a white speculum. The speculum, which is more obvious in flight, is bordered in front with a heavy band of black and then a patch of chestnut. The female has mottled brown plumage resembling that of female mallards, although smaller in size. The gadwall is often called "gray duck" because of the lack of striking colors. This dabbling duck eats mainly aquatic vegetation found in stagnant sloughs. It is occasionally seen in our area but there are no confirmed breeding records.

American Wigeon (35 cm)

BJKCKLWY

Anas americana

In his full breeding regalia, the American wigeon is a handsome duck. He has a white crown, marked by a bold slash of iridescent green extending from the eye to the nape, with the remainder of the head and neck speckled with black and white. Another good field mark is the large, white shoulder patch on the forewing followed by a greenish speculum which is bordered by black. The hen's plumage consists of warm shades of mottled brown. Her forewing, in contrast to that of the drake's, has a poorly defined whitish area. Their short, bluish bill has a black tip. Other common names such as "baldpate" and "bluebill" are derived from the shining white crown of the breeding male or from the blue bill. In the spring the male has a soft, mellow whistle *"whew,"* usually sounded in a group of three. These ducks are occasional breeders in our area.

Canvasback (38 cm)

BJKCLWY

Aythya valisineria

The largest of the diving ducks, canvasbacks, or "cans" as they are often called, are an open-water species. The breeding male has a rust red head, the color continuing to the shoulders, a black breast and rear end, and a canvas-colored back. Although closely resembling the redhead, the canvasback can be distinguished by its more substantial black bill, longer neck, wedge-shaped head, larger size, and paler gray back. The adult female is similar in size but with a pale brown back and reddish brown head, neck, and chest. Males in eclipse plumage are similar to females. The feet projecting somewhat beyond the tail in flight is a good field mark. Their principal food is tuberous roots of aquatic plants, often secured at depths of 1 to 4 m. After the breeding and rearing season, these gregarious ducks congregate in large flotillas or rafts well out on the lake to sleep, rest, and feed. Because of its large size and small wings, the canvasback patters along the surface of the water for some distance before becoming airborne. Once airborne, it is one of the most powerful flyers among ducks, capable of speeds of more than 100 km/h. They appear to be only migrants in the Rockies.

Gadwall (male)

American Wigeon (male and female)

Canvasback (male)

Redhead (37 cm)   BJKCKLWY
Aythya americana   WATERFOWL FAMILY

Redheads, large diving ducks, are often confused with canvasbacks. They share
the same habitats and their plumage is similar. The adult breeding male is a
large, gray-backed, white-breasted duck with a brick red head and upper neck,
and a black lower neck and chest. The rounded head of the redhead in contrast to
the wedge-shaped head of the canvasback, easily separates them. The adult
female is a brown-backed, white-breasted bird with a yellowish brown head and
whitish chin. Both sexes have short, broad, tricolored bills and pearl gray wing
patches. The bill is mostly pale blue with a narrow white ring bordering a black
tip. In our area, drakes in eclipse plumage, immature birds, and females can be
confused with canvasbacks, ring-necked ducks, and lesser scaup. The voice of the
adult male is an unique catlike *"mee-ow"* sound. Redheads feed by diving in
water 1 to 4 m deep, consuming a high proportion of plant material. Although
redheads pass through the Canadian Rockies during the spring and fall, there are
no nesting records.

Ring-necked Duck (30 cm)   . BJKCKLWY
Aythya collaris   WATERFOWL FAMILY

The drake ring-neck is a chunky duck with a black head, neck, breast, and back.
White crescents in front of the wings separate its black breast from gray sides.
Close observations may reveal a wash of purple on the head and neck and a gloss
of green on the breast. His bill is a drab slate with a white band just before the
black tip and at the base. The head has a crest which gives it a topheavy
appearance and an entirely different contour. An inconspicuous chestnut collar,
for which the species is named, is a poor field mark. Females are brown with
pale cheeks and a prominent white eye-ring and white line or bridle extending
back from the eye. In flight, the ring-necked duck can be separated from the
lesser scaup by the gray instead of flashing white speculum. In addition, the
lesser scaup has a lighter-barred back and grayer flanks. This is a shallow diving
duck, usually feeding in water 50 cm to 150 cm deep. Predominantly vegetarians,
they eat tubers, pondweeds, and large quantities of seeds. They are fairly
common in the Canadian Rockies.

Lesser Scaup (30 cm)   BJKCKLWY
Aythya affinis   WATERFOWL FAMILY

The lesser scaup, or "bluebill" as it is often called by hunters, is a large duck
with a glossy black head, neck, and foreparts, a bluish bill, and finely flecked
flanks that appear white at a distance. In good light you may see that the head
and neck are masked with a hint of purple. The hen is generally brown with a
bold white face patch at the base of the bill. Although in no hurry to return north
in the spring, they linger in the fall until the last water is frozen. Scaup, with
their large and powerful feet, are expert divers. They nest on the borders of
marshes and ponds in the Canadian Rockies but are most often seen in the open
water of larger lakes. They are deep-water feeders, diving for a wealth of aquatic
insects and plants.

Redhead (male and female)

Ring-necked Duck

Lesser Scaup

Harlequin Duck (30 cm)

BJKCKWY

Histrionicus histrionicus

WATERFOWL FAMILY

The male harlequin is an unmistakable bird marked with a gaudy plumage of blues, russets, blacks, and whites. White markings on the head and neck include crescents in front of and over the eyes, a spot behind the ears, a stripe down the side of the neck, and a ring around the base of the neck. That decorated pattern and elegant form, like the masked character of comedy and pantomime, have given rise to its name. The female, in contrast, is dark brown marked by three whitish spots on both sides of the head. The cold water of mountain streams and lakes is the summer home of this beautiful duck. The harlequin is a diving sea duck from along rocky coasts that migrates to the mountains to court, mate, and produce its young. They are expert swimmers taking little apparent notice of the tumbling waters as they dive under the strongest currents or brawling glacial streams. The male returns to the seacoast, leaving the female to raise the young. A few harlequins are reported to winter on open water at the outlet of Maligne Lake in Jasper National Park.

Oldsquaw (38 cm)

BJKCLW

Clangula hyemalis

WATERFOWL FAMILY

An oldsquaw male has conspicuous, long tail feathers that can be mistaken only for the northern pintail, but it has a smaller, chunky body with entirely different markings. In the spring and summer the adult male has a dark brown head, neck, breast, and back with white flanks and lower abdomen. They have neatly rounded heads, small, pink-banded bills, and short necks. Lacking the long tail feathers, the females are mottled brown with dark, smudged heads. Oldsquaws are essentially a sea duck and come inland for the breeding season. This arctic breeding duck, with a circumpolar distribution, is better known as the "long-tailed duck" in some regions. It is a fairly common migrant in the northern portion of the Canadian Rockies, passing through from mid-April to mid-May.

Surf Scoter

BJKCKLWY

Melanitta perspicillata

WATERFOWL FAMILY

The male surf scoter is all black except for a white triangle on the forehead and another on the nape pointing downward. Its bill—a mosaic of white, red, yellow, and black—has a swollen base and is elevated along the ridge, abruptly descending over the nostrils. Females are dark brown, even darker on the back, with pale patches on the head. A paired male ensures the bonding is maintained by making short flights on slowly beating wings that produce a whistling sound as he passes the female. He then lands and stretches his neck and wings upward as the mate swims or flies to him. Both sexes lack the white wing patches that separate them easily from the white-winged scoter. They have sloping, not rounded, foreheads. These birds are occasionally seen on lakes in both the spring and fall from Banff northward and they likely breed in the northern portion of the Canadian Rockies.

Harlequin Duck (male and female)

Oldsquaw

Surf Scoter (male)

23

White-winged Scoter (40 cm)
Melanitta fusca

The white-winged scoter is easy to recognize in any season by its all black or dark plumage with pronounced white patches on the hindwing. Adult males have a black knob at the base of a colorful beak that is orange at the tip. It has white crescent-shaped patches extending backward from below the white eyes. Females are a dark sooty brown with two vague whitish marks near their brown eyes. Their bills are black and lack the swollen base of the males. During the spring and fall migrations these ducks are fairly common on large lakes and are often seen sitting on open water in rafts of various sizes. These birds likely breed in the northern portion of the Rockies.

Common Goldeneye (33 cm)
Bucephala clangula

Because of the characteristic musical whistle heard in takeoff or in flight, the common goldeneye is often called "whistler." The *"woo woo woo"* sound is not vocal but is produced by their wings during flight. This sound of nature is one of the earliest to be heard in the spring because the common goldeneye arrives with the first suggestion of breakup and is one of the last to leave in the autumn. Occasionally they overwinter on lakes and rivers in the southern portion of the Canadian Rockies. The male is a striking black-and-white duck with yellow eyes. It differs from the male Barrow's goldeneye by having an iridescent greenish wash on the head rather than purple, an oval instead of crescentic white face mark as well as considerably more white on the wings and back pattern. The female is light colored with a contrasting brown head. After an elaborate courtship the female looks for an old hollow snag, large woodpecker hole, or a cavity in a tree to nest. After the eggs hatch, she calls her chicks to leave the hole and they "parachute" 2 to 10 m to the ground. They also take readily to suitably erected nestboxes. They are known to breed only in the northern portion of our area.

Barrow's Goldeneye (33 cm)
Bucephala islandica

Secluded mountain lakes and ponds where forests crowd the water's edge are preferred summer habitats for Barrow's goldeneye. By April many mountain ponds will have a courting flock of these birds. The males, their heads puffed out to the greatest possible extent, swim and bow toward a receptive female. These males frequently give a backward kick that is strong enough to send a jet of water skyward. The males closely resemble common goldeneye except for the purplish gloss on the black head, the white crescent below the golden eye, a finger of black on the side of the chest, and less white on the back in the form of spots instead of streaks. This species is a tree-nester using cavities in decaying trunks that are close to water. After incubation the black-and-white balls of fluff soon jump to the ground in quick succession, following mom to water and staying with her for about two months. These birds are common north of Banff and less common to the south.

E. JONES

White-winged Scoter (male)

T. ULRICH

Common Goldeneye (male and female)

T. ULRICH

Barrow's Goldeneye (male)

25

Bufflehead (25 cm)   BJKCKLWY
Bucephala albeola   WATERFOWL FAMILY

About the same size as a teal, the bufflehead, or "butterball" as some hunters call it, is the smallest diving duck in the Canadian Rockies. Adult males are black above and white below with pinkish legs and feet. Their black heads, with a purple-and-green sheen, are puffy in appearance and marked with a bald patch of white that extends from the eyes to across the top of the head like a shawl. In contrast, females and first-year males are dark brown above with barred, gray-buff underparts. An obvious field mark on the female is a small white comma mark behind and below the eye. Bufflehead males do not breed or obtain adult plumage until they are nearly two years old. The most common of the courtship displays is a jerky head-bobbing action by the drake with his head moving forward and then way back over the tail. An upward stretch with wing flapping terminates most displays. The bufflehead is the only tree-nesting duck small enough to use nestholes of the common flicker. Shortly after hatching the young jump to the ground, 3 to 15 m below, and follow their mother to the nearest water. These birds can be seen on lakes, marshes, and rivers from April to November. They breed in the Canadian Rockies.

Hooded Merganser (33 cm)   BJKCKWY
Lophodytes cucullatus   WATERFOWL FAMILY

The hooded merganser is the smallest of the mergansers. A breeding male is black above and cinnamon below with a white breast. The black-and-white, fan-shaped crest gives the bird a large-headed appearance as well as its name. Raising or lowering the crest can dramatically change the amount of white showing and the shape of the head. The tertiaries have long white stripes and the secondaries show much white. Females have a tawny brown head and upper neck with an orange-buff crest that is seldom raised. Their upperparts are dark grayish brown, paler below. Hooded mergansers are secretive birds preferring shady streams, small ponds, and marshes surrounded by forest for their breeding habitat. They are cavity-nesting birds, often using old woodpecker holes in trees near the water. Although there are nesting records from the late 1800s for Waterton and Banff national parks, this merganser is usually seen as a migrant in the spring, late summer, and fall.

Bufflehead (male)

Hooded Merganser (male)

Hooded Merganser (female)

27

Common Merganser (45 cm)

BJKCKLWY
WATERFOWL FAMILY

Mergus merganser

At a distance, male common mergansers, or "fish ducks" as they are often called, appear black and white. They have dark blackish green heads with black backs, and white on the necks and undersides. Female and young have silvery gray on their backs, reddish brown heads with tufted feathers that give a distinctly angular profile, and white undersides. The adaptation that makes them successful fishing birds is a long, narrow bill edged with sawlike "teeth," hence the nickname "sawbill." The bill and feet are distinctly red. Among the earliest ducks to fly north in spring, common mergansers arrive in nesting grounds as soon as the ice begins to melt. Preferred habitat is most often in boreal-forested areas near streams or marshy bays where small fishes, a staple in their diet, are plentiful. Nests are built in tree cavities, in bluffs, and along rocky shorelines where trees are not abundant. They are often recognized by the way they fly in long, trailing lines slightly above the water, and by the exhausting run along the water required to get their heavy bodies aloft. These mergansers are common breeding birds in the Canadian Rockies, particularly in the southern portion.

Red-breasted Merganser (40 cm)

BJKCKLWY
WATERFOWL FAMILY

Mergus serrator

A male red-breasted is distinguished from the common merganser by a shaggy double crest, white collar, and streaked reddish band across the breast. The female's head and neck are paler than the female common merganser. Like other fish-eating ducks it has a thin, highly serrated bill armed with "teeth" to grip slippery prey. Breeding in the tundra and boreal zones, the red-breasted merganser has a circumpolar distribution. Red-breasted mergansers are fairly rare in the southern portion of the Canadian Rockies, increasing in numbers on lakes and rivers from Jasper northward. They are primarily spring migrants except for the extreme northern portion of the Rockies where they are summer residents.

Common Merganser

Red-breasted Merganser (male)

Red-breasted Merganser (female)

Ruddy Duck

Oxyura jamaicensis

WATERFOWL FAMILY

In breeding plumage the male ruddy duck is rufous chestnut on the flanks, back, and neck. From its crown to below the eye and nape is black with a prominent white chin and cheek patch. His broad bill is a sky blue with a peculiar hook to the nail. During the breeding season he bustles importantly before his dull-colored mate with his beak pressed against his breast and his black tail cocked up like a spread fan over his back. During the stiff-tail display the bold white undertail coverts are often visible. Both sexes have a round, chunky body with a short, thick neck. The female is dressed in plain browns, darkest on the crown, with a dark horizontal line through the white facial patch. She carries her tail down, often invisible at water level. In the Canadian Rockies the ruddy duck is an occasional migrant during the spring and autumn.

Osprey (57 cm)

Pandion haliaetus

BJKCKLWY

HAWK FAMILY

The large size and distinctive plumage distinguish the osprey from other hawks. Adults are dark brown on the upper body with contrasting white on the forehead, neck, chin, and underparts. A black stripe passes through the eye and down the side of the neck. Living almost exclusively on fish, the osprey is usually found near sizable bodies of water. Although this "fish hawk" is not a deep diver, it can take fish in water as deep as 1 m. They catch their meal in a spectacular way. Osprey typically fly 10 to 30 m over the water scanning for fish. When a fish is sighted, the bird hovers, folds its wings upward and backward, thrusts its feet forward, and plunges feet first into the water with a resounding splash. Captured fish are carried headfirst to a feeding perch or to the nest. The osprey is especially adapted to fish catching. It has an opposable outer toe and sharp specules on the bottom of the feet for holding slippery fish. Ospreys usually choose nesting sites near or over water. The nest is a bulky structure built mostly of sticks in the top of trees, power and telephone poles, and artificial nest platforms. Nests may be used year after year. Ospreys are fairly common breeding birds in the Rockies.

Ruddy Duck (male and female)

Osprey

Osprey

31

Bald Eagle (82 cm)

Haliaeetus leucocephalus

BJKCKLWY

With its prominent white head and tail, hooked beak, deeply carved talons, and 2-m wingspread, the bald eagle is truly an impressive bird, one of the largest in the Canadian Rockies. The eagle's preferred habitat is near water, especially larger lakes or rivers. They feed on carrion, ducks, catch live fish close enough to the surface to be seized with their talons, or harry successful osprey until their catch is dropped. As a mating display, a pair may lock their feet together in flight and tumble earthward for several turns before releasing. Bald eagles generally have two young reared in a tree nest that may be 2 m across. These great clumps of sticks may be used year after year. Parents mate for life and share the duties of raising their offspring. Juveniles do not acquire the white head and tail until about three years of age. This national emblem of the United States is fairly common in the Canadian Rockies, sometimes spending the whole year there.

Northern Harrier (42 cm)

Circus cyaneus

BJKCKLWY

HAWK FAMILY

Formerly called "marsh hawk," the northern harrier in all ages and both sexes has a conspicuous white rump patch and a partial facial disk. It is a medium-sized hawk with a long, slender build. The adult male is slate gray above and white below with black wing tips. Females are brown above and whitish or buffy white below with brown streaks. Immatures of both sexes are dark brown above and rich rusty brown below with lighter streaking than the adult female. When soaring, this harrier holds its wings decidedly elevated above the body instead of almost horizontal as other hawks do. They hunt by flying low over meadows and marshes, with alternating flaps and glides. Their diet consists primarily of birds, insects, and mice. They nest on the ground among grasses and low bushes. When the male carries prey toward the nest during incubation, the female rises to meet her mate and the food is transferred by a mid-air catch. Although the northern harrier is fairly common in the Canadian Rockies during migration, the only breeding records are from the Waterton area and the foothills.

Bald Eagle (mature)　　　　*Bald Eagle (immature)*

Northern Harrier (male)

33

Sharp-shinned Hawk (27 cm)

BJKCKLWY

Accipiter striatus

HAWK FAMILY

The sharp-shinned hawk is found in mixed woodlands where it nests and finds its prey. This bird pursues its prey, which is made up largely of small birds, by dashing among the trees, not by watching for prey while soaring on air currents. The sharp-shinned hawk's pursuit of prey can be so relentless that it may smack full force into thickets or tree branches. Its diet consists primarily of small birds but insects, mice, and other small forest animals are taken, also. Adults have dark blue upperparts and barred reddish brown and white abdomens and breasts. The sharp-shinned is very similar to the Cooper's hawk, except that the former has a square-tipped tail compared with the slightly round tail of the latter. Sharp-shinned hawks breed throughout the Canadian Rockies and occasionally overwinter in the central and southern portions.

Cooper's Hawk (40 cm)

BJKCKWY

Accipiter cooperii

HAWK FAMILY

In appearance the Cooper's hawk is a look-alike of the sharp-shinned hawk, except that the tail on Cooper's is longer and round-tipped rather than square. Cooper's hawks are generally larger in size and adults have a more prominent contrast between the almost black crown and slate gray back. The two species, however, are easily confused. Not only do they look alike, but they prefer the same habitat. Cooper's hawks give a large number of calls or variations, but the most common is a cackling *"ca-ca-ca-ca"* with a harsh staccato quality. They hunt at low levels in the forests catching both birds and small mammals. Their short wingspan is well adapted for quick maneuvering in deep woods. It breeds throughout the southern half of the Rockies.

Northern Goshawk (48 cm)

BJKCKLWY

Accipiter gentilis

HAWK FAMILY

The largest of the three accipiters in our area, the northern goshawk's size allows it to kill quite large game. Its favorite foods are ruffed grouse and snowshoe hares, but various other birds and mammals are taken also. They are fierce, aggressive, and very persistent in pursuing prey. Northern goshawks are the only short-winged hawk regularly trained for falconry and they are regarded as efficient killers. Adult birds are a dark blue-gray above; underparts are white with gray barrings. The light stripe over the eye is a good field mark at close range. This hawk is a bird of forests and woodlands, preferring mixedwoods and forest edges. The male is a good "family man." He builds the nest and supplies the food. Northern goshawks are very aggressive and will attack humans who venture too near their nest. They breed throughout the Canadian Rockies and are year-round residents in the southern half of our area.

Sharp-shinned Hawk

Cooper's Hawk

Northern Goshawk

Swainson's Hawk (45 cm)

BJKCKWY

Buteo swainsoni

HAWK FAMILY

The Swainson's hawk is a common buteo, or soaring hawk, of open grasslands and prairies. Plumage of adults shows a bewildering variety of coloration. A bird of the light phase has a dark breast, pale wing linings, dark flight feathers, and a gray tail shading to white at the base. Dark phase birds have a darkish body and wings with a barred tail that is gray. There is also a rufous phase. Regardless of the coloration, it never has a reddish uppertail like the red-tailed hawk. In addition, the Swainson's hawk has a concentration of dark markings across the breast instead of across the abdomen as is common with red-tailed hawks. It can also be distinguished from the red-tailed by having three instead of four notched primaries. The Swainson's call is a long, whistled *"kree-ee-ee-ee,"* less harsh than that of the red-tailed. Richardson's ground squirrels, mice, and grasshoppers are the principle foods of this hawk. Swainson's hawks are occasional visitors in the foothills of the Rockies.

Red-tailed Hawk (46 cm)

BJKCKLWY

Buteo jamaicensis

HAWK FAMILY

Like other members of the buteo family, the red-tailed hawk is large, thick-bodied, and broad-winged. The plumage variations of western red-tailed hawks are so extreme that color characteristics make identification uncertain. They are best distinguished from Swainson's by having light flight feathers in all plumages. The red-tailed hawk has a dark area across the abdomen, with a lighter breast. In Swainson's the lightest spot is below the breast. The reddish uppertail, spread wide in flight, is not always determinative of this species. Immatures and some races of this hawk lack the red tail. "Red-tails" are adept at soaring, often circling aloft for hours. When soaring the wings are held horizontally, in contrast to the somewhat upward tilt of the Swainson's hawk. The red-tailed's usual call is a shrill and rasping *"tsee-eeee-arrr"* scream. Although opportunistic feeders, they are inveterate mouse-eaters. They are a common hawk of parklands and mixedwood forests and nest throughout the Canadian Rockies at low elevations.

Rough-legged Hawk (48 cm)

BJKCKLWY

Buteo lagopus

HAWK FAMILY

Plumage of the rough-legged hawk is extremely variable including light, intermediate, and dark phases. However, the long white tail with a dark band or multibands identifies this species in all plumages. A dark body band from the waist down is a good identification mark. As well, it has a black patch at the bend of the wing on the underside and a small white patch at the base of the primaries on the upperwings. It has a habit of hovering in the air over one spot. All the food is caught on the ground, either by a short stoop from a perch or by dropping on it from a hover. Mice, ground squirrels, and rabbits form the principle portion of their diet. The rough-legged hawk, nesting in the arctic and subarctic, is an occasional spring and fall migrant through the Canadian Rockies.

Swainson's Hawk

G. JONES

Red-tailed Hawk

T. ULRICH

Rough-legged Hawk

Golden Eagle (81 cm)

Aquila chrysaetos

HAWK FAMILY

This bird derives its common name from the golden buff feathers of the hindneck. All other parts of mature birds are dark brown except for the lighter basal portion of the tail and the white underwing patches that can be seen in flight. The end of the tail is dark, but the coverts at the base are obscurely mottled or barred with gray. Juvenile birds are dark brown with a prominent white spot at the base of the primaries on both the upper and lower surfaces; their tail is largely white with a broad black border. Although difficult to see in the field, the fully feathered legs of the golden eagle are diagnostic and separate it from the bald eagle. The golden eagle is a bird of the mountains, often seen soaring effortlessly for hours over alpine meadows and mountain ridges. Pairs mate for life and usually nest on cliffs, but occasionally in trees. Their diet shows a strong preference for mammals such as ground squirrels, hares, and marmots. They breed throughout the Canadian Rockies.

Golden Eagle

Golden Eagle (immature)

Golden Eagle

American Kestrel (22 cm)

BJKCKLWY

Falco sparverius

FALCON FAMILY

The American kestrel is the smallest and most common falcon in the Canadian Rockies. They are also the most gayly colored with rufous-barred backs, rufous tails, and striking double black stripes on the white face. The tail of the female is banded with black while the male's is only black tipped. The male has blue-gray wings. Both sexes have the falcon characteristics of long, slender, pointed wings and long, narrow tail. Thankfully, the former misleading name of "sparrow hawk" has been replaced. Insects, especially grasshoppers, and mice are staples in the diet, not sparrows or other small birds. Like all falcons they eat only freshly killed food. Kestrels prefer to hunt over open country, often using vantage points such as powerline poles and lines, fenceposts, or treetops. Their call is a high-pitched and often repeated *"killy-killy-killy."* They nest throughout the Rockies, often choosing abandoned holes of flickers and other woodpeckers.

Merlin (30 cm)

BJKCKLWY

Falco columbarius

FALCON FAMILY

Male merlins are blue-gray above and the females are brown. Both sexes have creamy breasts and abdomens heavily streaked with browns. They lack the strong facial pattern and reddish upperparts of the American kestrel. At rest, their long, pointed wings extend almost to the tip of the tail. The merlins' strongly barred, black-and-white tails distinguish them from other falcons. "Pigeon hawks," as they were formerly called, are swift flyers, coursing immediately above copses of trees and snatching small birds and insects out of the air. They seize prey by sudden bursts of speed rather than by diving. Merlins are a rather scarce bird throughout the Rockies, generally preferring open forests and lakeshore habitats in the subalpine region. They often use abandoned tree nests of other birds, such as those of the crow or magpie, for nesting.

Peregrine Falcon (45 cm)

BJKCLW

Falco peregrinus

FALCON FAMILY

One of the most magnificent of all birds, the peregrine falcon is a victim of man's indiscriminate use of toxic pesticides. The peregrine has become a conservation symbol and an early warning to man as to the state of our shared environment. This crow-sized bird is distinguished from other falcons by its black, crowned head and distinctive, black, mustachelike markings on its pale-colored neck and throat. Its back, tail, and wings are dark blue-gray in color, and its pale abdomen is barred with dark gray-brown. Peregrines are extremely powerful and agile fliers. The most spectacular part of a peregrine falcon's flight is called a "stoop" or a dive. It literally tucks in its wings and falls like a guided missile attaining blistering speeds of 250 km/h. At the bottom of the dive, it quickly spreads its wings and levels out overtaking its prey and delivering a fatal blow with its talons. Peregrines exist on a diet of birds ranging from small passerines to those goose-sized. Although the peregrine falcon is now very rare in the Rockies, it is to be hoped that man's recent activities can restore this noble bird to its former abundance.

American Kestrel

Peregrine Falcon

Merlin

Gyrfalcon (55 cm)   BJKC
Falco rusticolus   FALCON FAMILY

Breeding in the Arctic, the gyrfalcon is a very rare but spectacularly beautiful
visitor to the Canadian Rockies. Its plumage can be mostly white, almost solidly
black, or any intermediate between these extremes. In the light phase it may bear
a strong resemblance to a snowy owl, but is easily identified by its smaller head,
narrower pointed wings, and quicker wingbeats. Darker birds may be confused
with immature peregrine falcons, but the mustache stripe is obscure or lacking.
Tails of "gyrs" may be barred or unbarred. In the past, the use of gyrs in
falconry was reserved for royalty. When hunting they tend to fly fast and near the
ground to flush prey, which is then pursued with great speed and power. Their
diet is chiefly birds during the winter and ground squirrels during their summer
in the Arctic.

Prairie Falcon (40 cm)   BJKCW
Falco mexicanus   FALCON FAMILY

Unlike the peregrine falcon, which kills only in flight, the prairie falcon feeds
partly on ground-dwelling mammals and insects and partly on birds taken in
flight. The prairie falcon is a pale brown or sandy-colored falcon. The single best
field mark in flight is the blackish patch where the wing meets the underbody.
Adult birds have a whitish line over the eye and a much less prominent dark
brown mustache streak than the peregrine. Their streamlined, missile-shaped
bodies and pointed wings allow them to make spectacular aerial dives as part of a
mating ritual or in the pursuit of prey. The call of the prairie falcon is a shrill
yelping *"kik-kik-kik,"* which is often repeated. While not known to breed in the
Rockies, the prairie falcon is occasionally seen in the mountains from Jasper
south.

Gray Partridge (32 cm)   BJKCW
Perdix perdix   GROUSE FAMILY

This little foreigner was introduced to Alberta from Europe in 1908. The
population increased rapidly and it is an abundant bird in the central and
southern portion of that province. The gray partridge is a small, brownish bird
with a rusty face and throat. Males have a rich chestnut, horseshoe-shaped mark
on the belly. The reddish tail is obvious and distinctive in flight. Other than
during the nesting season, this partridge is very gregarious and lives in a covey of
several birds. When a covey is flushed they rise with a whir of wings and a rapid
cackle, generally flying and gliding just above the ground. "Hungarian
partridges" or "huns," as they are often called, thrive in cultivated habitats and
open grasslands. They have a very high reproductive potential with up to twenty
plain brown eggs to a nest. Nests are a scrape in the ground, often sheltered by
grass or low shrubs. "Huns" are seen occasionally in the foothills of the Rockies.

Gyrfalcon (white phase)

T. ULRICH

Gyrfalcon (gray phase)

Prairie Falcon

A. NELSON

Gray Partridge

Spruce Grouse (33 cm)

BJKCKLWY

Dendragapus canadensis

GROUSE FAMILY

A permanent resident of the coniferous forests, the spruce grouse is widely distributed throughout the Canadian Rockies. The male can be identified by its dark throat and breast which are edged in white, a white line behind the eye, and a scarlet comb of bare skin above the eye. In the southern Canadian Rockies, the male differs by having a black tail (no brown tips) with broad, white-tipped uppertail coverts. During the mating season, the strutting male with red comb inflated and tail erect and spread is a beautiful sight. Upperparts of the adult female are irregularly barred with black, gray, and rust and the underparts are barred black, white, and rust. The nest, lined with grasses and leaves, is a shallow depression in the ground, often under the protective branches of a conifer. Usually four to ten in number, the eggs are light brown and handsomely marked with dark brown. Spruce grouse feed on conifer needles and buds during the winter and berries of different sorts when they are available. Ridiculously tame, the spruce grouse can be closely approached and studied, or killed with a stick or stone. This habit has earned them another name—"fool hen."

Blue Grouse (43 cm)

BJKCKLWY

Dendragapus obscurus

GROUSE FAMILY

During the spring a series of hoots may emerge from the conifer forests of the subalpine zone. Careful investigation will trace this sound to a cock blue grouse displaying in his territory. He attracts the female with a series of sounds which are produced by the inflation of throat sacs, which amplifies his hootings. The courtship display also involves strutting in front of the female with tail fanned, body tipped forward, and wings touching the ground. That display may be preceded by a fluttering above the ground or by a short, circular flight. The cock's sooty gray plumage is set off by yellow-orange combs above each eye and white, downy feathers that fringe the reddish to purple throat sacs. Its mate is a mottled brown above with a plain gray belly. Both sexes have dark tails. Blue grouse are fairly common year-round residents in the Canadian Rockies, preferring coniferous forests near treeline, avalanche slopes, and burns as habitats. They feed on fruits, berries, and insects when available and on pine needles during the winter.

Spruce Grouse

Blue Grouse

Blue Grouse (displaying)

45

Willow Ptarmigan (33 cm)　　　　　　　　　　　　　　　　　J
Lagopus lagopus　　　　　　　　　　　　　　　　　　　　GROUSE FAMILY

Ptarmigan (pronounced TAR-mi-gun) have chunky bodies, short, rounded wings, and short tails, much like other grouse. Their short legs and toes are feathered. The snowshoelike feathering of the toes improves the ptarmigan's ability to walk in loose snow. The winter dress of willow ptarmigan is basically pure white except for the beak, eyes, and black tail feathers. The summer plumage of the male is chestnut faintly barred with black on the head, neck, back, and breast. A scarlet comb over the eye is prominent in the spring and early summer. Females, in the summer, are heavily barred with dark brown and ochre. Willow ptarmigan are fairly common permanent residents in the alpine areas from Jasper northward. They feed on leaves, buds, and flowers during the summer and on willow, birch, and alder buds during the winter. During extremely cold winter storms the birds burrow into the snow for protection. Unlike the white-tailed, the male willow ptarmigan helps in rearing the brood of six to ten chicks.

White-tailed Ptarmigan (25 cm)　　　　　　　　　BJKCKLWY
Lagopus leucurus　　　　　　　　　　　　　　　　　　　GROUSE FAMILY

The white-tailed ptarmigan, another permanent mountain resident, is found at high elevations. In the winter it is entirely white except for the dark beak, eyes, and red eye-comb. Even the legs and toes of the bird are completely feathered. In summer, the body of the white-tailed ptarmigan is a mottled brown or black with a white tail, wings, and belly. The spring and fall molts create a patchy brownish white appearance. The white tail distinguishes it from the willow ptarmigan, found in Jasper and farther north, which has a black tail. The protective coloration allows the bird to blend perfectly with the surrounding vegetation and rocks. These birds are so well camouflaged and so unwary that you practically have to step on them before they flush. Preferring alpine meadows and rock slopes above treeline, they nest in a depression in the ground sparsely lined with grasses, leaves, and feathers. There are usually four to eight eggs, which are buff with darker spots or blotches. Seeing a hen escorting her chicks across an alpine meadow is compensation for the climb to their habitat.

Willow Ptarmigan

White-tailed Ptarmigan (summer plumage)

White-tailed ptarmigan (winter plumage)

47

Ruffed Grouse

Bonasa umbellus

Have you heard the *"put-put-put-put-purrrrr"* of the male ruffed grouse or "drummer" on an early spring morning? It starts out slowly, but rapidly increases to a drumroll. Usually performed on a log, a series of strong wingstrokes compress the air, creating a vacuum to produce the thumping sound. The drumming is used to establish a territory and to attract females. A chickenlike bird, the body feathers of the ruffed grouse are mottled brown with light underparts. The ruff feathers on each side of the neck are usually iridescent black. They are displayed as an umbrella-like, large collar by the male during courtship or aggression. The feathers on top of the head may also be erected into a small crest. Color of the tail feathers varies from red to brown to gray. The broad band near the tip of the fan-shaped tail is usually black, but occasionally bronze. The sexes are similar in appearance except that the male has larger ruffs and tail. Males have a bright orange to salmon patch of face skin above the eye while that area is bluish gray to pale orange in females. Ruffed grouse are common year-round residents in the montane zone, particularly in aspen. Well adapted to winter, grouse have "snowshoes," lateral extensions of the scales of the toes, which help them travel over soft snow. They also roost in snow burrows to cope with extreme cold and for protection from predators.

Sharp-tailed Grouse (38 cm)

Tympanuchus phasianellus

The sharp-tailed grouse is a medium-sized brownish bird with a short, pointed tail. Its common name was derived from the two slightly elongated central tail feathers, which are mottled with brown, black, and white. The other tail feathers are white and are a good field mark when the bird is in flight. Feathers of the underparts are V-marked in black. "Sharp-tails" gather on dancing grounds during the spring breeding season to perform a courtship dance. During this period the male's yellow comb becomes enlarged and the purplish air sacs on the neck become inflated. The dance includes rapid stamping of the feet, ruffled feathers, lowered head, and a booming sound produced through the mouth by air released from the sacs. Each male defends his territory while trying to attract females for breeding. Sharp-tails prefer grasslands, parklands, and the edges of forest clearings as habitats. They are year-long residents of the foothills.

Ruffed Grouse (drumming)

Sharp-tailed Grouse

Sharp-tailed Grouse

Sora (17 cm)
Porzana carolina

BJKCKLWY
RAIL FAMILY

Very secretive, the sora is more often heard than seen. Its call is a series of plaintive notes gradually decreasing in tone and intensity and often followed by a maniacal laugh. This shy marsh bird has a stocky body, short wings, and long legs which dangle when flying short distances. A breeding male is brownish olive above with both coarse black and fine white streaks. Its face, center of the throat, and breast have black markings; the female is duller in color. Their thick bills and long legs are greenish yellow. The sora breeds, feeds, and nests in and around sloughs and shallow lakes throughout the Rockies.

American Coot (30 cm)
Fulica americana

BJKCKLWY
RAIL FAMILY

Often called "mudhen" or "whitebill," the American coot is a member of the rail family, not the duck family as many casual observers believe. Instead of a flat duck-bill, the coot sports a white, chickenlike bill which extends into the frontal shield of the forehead. In addition, coots have scallop-shaped lobes on the toes instead of webbed feet. They have a distinctive swimming motion with their heads bobbing back and forth as they paddle. Both sexes are identical "plain-Jane" birds, with slate gray plumage and white rumps. Coots are extremely aggressive and breeding territories are defended by both sexes. Both participate in nest building and incubation of the eggs. Newly hatched young have black downy bodies, red bills, and a thin cover of bristlelike orange down on the heads. The young cannot fend for themselves so they are fed by the parents. Coots are expert divers and can feed on succulent plants submerged well below the water surface. Although they are a common bird, particularly in the southern part of the Canadian Rockies, there are no breeding records.

Sora

American Coot

American Coot (young)

Sandhill Crane (104 cm)
Grus canadensis

The sandhill crane is a large bird, standing 1 m tall and having a wingspan of about 2 m. Achieving full adult plumage after two years, the birds are light gray in color with long legs, long necks, and bright red crowns. During migration they often fly at great heights, sometimes making wide circles as they ride the thermals. They fly with their necks outstretched, unlike great blue herons which fly with their necks folded back. Sandhills have a distinctive *"gor-oo-ooo"* call, often uttered in flight, that is audible over a great distance. The dance of the sandhills is one of the more remarkable performances in the natural world. While dancing, their long legs are used as springs to leap high in the air employing partially spread wings for balance. Although such displays are more common during the breeding season, they occur throughout the year. Sandhills feed in fields during the day, always returning to water at night. They are occasionally seen as migrants in the Rockies and they have nested near Rocky Mountain House.

Semipalmated Plover (13 cm)
Charadrius semipalmatus

Semipalmated plovers are occasional migrants in our area, frequenting both mud flats and sandy beaches of larger lakes as they rest and search for food. On landing they spread out over the shore running about with heads up or stabbing for invertebrates. Sandpipers, with which they often associate, remain close together with their heads down. When alarmed the scattered plovers fly off rapidly in a very close-knit flock. This plover is brown-backed with a well-defined single black band across the white breast and a black bar above the white forehead. It has a short orange bill with a black tip. The scientific name *semipalmatus* is derived from the partially webbed toes of this bird. Their call is a *"pee WIT,"* the second syllable higher pitched.

Killdeer (20 cm)
Charadrius vociferus

A member of the plover family, this noisy bird gets its common name from its *"kill-dee-deer"* call, which is repeated loud and often. The handsome killdeer has two distinctive markings, two black bands across the white chest as well as an orange-colored lower back, rump, and tail. The upper back and wings are brown with white wing stripes visible in flight. Killdeers are skilled actors, having developed an injury-feigning distraction when an intruder approaches their nest. The bird runs some distance from the nest, spreads and depresses its tail, holds up one wing, and drags itself along the ground while uttering a loud distress call. After decoying the intruder farther and farther from the nest the adult miraculously recovers and flies off. Nests, usually with three to five eggs or young, are little more than convenient depressions in the ground. Killdeer are common shorebirds and breed throughout the Canadian Rockies.

Sandhill Crane

Semipalmated Plover

Killdeer

Killdeer ("broken wing" display)

53

American Avocet (38 cm)
Recurvirostra americana

The American avocet is a showy and wonderfully graceful bird that is unmistakable. It is a large black-and-white wader with a cinnamon red head and neck. Pipestemlike blue legs allow this bird to probe the mud for food in deeper water than many other shorebirds. Avocets feed by sweeping their long, upcurved bills from side to side through the water, skimming the surface for insects and larvae. Its common call is a loud *"wheet."* This bird is characteristic of alkaline lakes and sloughs of the arid prairies, but occasionally it is seen in the Rockies from Banff southward.

Greater Yellowlegs (28 cm)
Tringa melanoleuca

The greater yellowlegs is a large wader with a fine pattern of black-and-white plumage except for conspicuous uppertail coverts that are white. It has long yellow legs. Almost identical in coloration is the lesser yellowlegs (*Tringa flavipe*), which is best separated by its smaller size. Similar in appearance, habitat, and flight, the yellowlegs are most readily distinguishable by size when the two are together, as often happens. Greater yellowlegs also have a proportionately longer bill, thicker at the base and usually with a slight upturn at the tip. On the ground, both yellowlegs have a frequent nodding and teetering habit. It is started by a backward jerk of the head and then a nod with an upward tilting of the tail. Their calls are slightly different. Greater Yellowlegs give three or more *"tew"* notes in a slightly descending series. Lessers have a higher call of one to three *"tew"* notes. Both species are fairly common in the northern portion of the Rockies and are occasional migrants in the south. There are breeding records for the greater yellowlegs in Banff and Jasper.

Solitary Sandpiper (22 cm)
Tringa solitaria

The solitary sandpiper has a dark brown back that is finely speckled with white and heavily spotted with buffy white. Its lower throat, breast, and sides are streaked with blackish brown; the belly is white. White eye-rings and a lack of white eyelines will differentiate it from other sandpipers. In contrast to the yellowlegs, it has green-gray legs, a dark-centered tail with barred outer tail feathers, and dark wing linings. The solitary has nodding motions similar to the yellowlegs but different from the spotted sandpiper in that the bobs involve mainly the front of the body instead of the rear. As the name implies, this sandpiper is usually seen in twos or threes or very small flocks even during migration. The female uses a discarded tree nest for incubating her eggs. The solitary sandpiper is fairly common on the shores of small stagnant pools and streams at all elevations. It is less common in the southern portion of the Rockies.

T. ULRICH

American Avocet

E. JONES

Greater Yellowlegs

E. JONES

Solitary Sandpiper

55

Spotted Sandpiper (16 cm)

BJKCKLWY

Actitis macularia

SANDPIPER FAMILY

Probably the best-known shorebird in North America, the spotted sandpiper has round black spots on its whitish underparts from the neck to the tail during the breeding season. The upperparts are grayish brown with black bars. Its call is a sharp *"peet-weet."* The behavior of the "spotty" identifies it more accurately than color or voice. It constantly bobs its tail up and down by flexing its legs. This peculiar motion is called teetering. When spooked, the bird will flutter from the shore low over the water in a wide arc with wings stiffly downcurved and vibrating. The wings appear not to rise above the bird's lower body. The white bars on the wings are visible only in flight. The nest is a saucer-shaped depression in the ground, often lined with grass and moss. Males do most incubating of the eggs and caring for the young. They feed along margins of water bodies, preferring rocky and pebbly shorelines to mud flats because they catch insects on the wing or on the ground rather than probing for them in the mud. The spotted sandpiper is fairly common throughout the Canadian Rockies.

Upland Sandpiper (25 cm)

BJKCLWY

Bartramia longicauda

SANDPIPER FAMILY

Although the upland sandpiper is a shorebird, it is no great lover of water, preferring upland grassland habitats. This sandpiper has a slender neck, rounded head, and dark Vs on the buffy foreneck and breast. In flight the dark primaries contrast with the mottled brown upperparts. The bill is about as long as the head. When landing on a post or a treetop they hold their wings raised over the back before folding them into place. These birds live chiefly on insects, especially grasshoppers. The upland sandpiper has a very irregular and local distribution during the breeding season. It is scarce in the Rockies, but is known to breed in the foothills and mountains on occasion.

Semipalmated Sandpiper (13 cm)

BJY

Calidris pusilla

SANDPIPER FAMILY

The semipalmated sandpiper is a sparrow-sized shorebird. The black feathers on the upperparts have buffy margins. There are light lines over the eyes. It is similar in appearance to the least sandpiper, differing only by having black legs, a slightly thicker bill, and paler upperparts. The partial webbing of the toes gave rise to the common name "semipalmated." They sometimes stop for a few days rest during spring and fall migrations around lakes and sloughs where the shore extends into sandy beaches and mud flats. There they spread out along the shoreline feeding on small insects from the wet soil. They are most common on the eastern slope of the central and northern Rockies.

Spotted Sandpiper

Upland Sandpiper

Semipalmated Sandpiper

Least Sandpiper (12 cm)
Calidris minutilla

BJKCKLY
SANDPIPER FAMILY

Although not the best identifying characteristic, the least sandpiper is the smallest of the peeps. Reliable field marks include a slightly drooped black bill and distinctive yellow legs and feet. With a bird in hand, the unwebbed toes will distinguish the least from the semipalmated sandpiper. It is also more ruddy above with a darker buff breast than the latter, with which it can be confused. After nesting in the subarctic, large flocks stop to feed on mud flats and sandy shores of lakes before continuing their migration. When flushed by an intruder they take flight as a compact unit, only to alight farther along the shore. In flight they twist and turn in a zigzag course, all changing directions at the same instant. Although rather common in the central and northern portion of the Rockies during fall migrations, these birds are uncommon in the south.

Baird's Sandpiper (15 cm)
Calidris bairdii

BJKCKLY
SANDPIPER FAMILY

Other than its larger size the Baird's is very similar to the least and semipalmated sandpipers. It has a buff breast like the former and black legs like the latter. The Baird's has a larger and longer bill than the least sandpiper. The back of the Baird's has a scaly appearance, the rounded feathers being broadly edged with buff. The breast is generally a darker buff than the semipalmated sandpiper. Unlike the semipalmated, the tip of its folded wings extends beyond the tip of the tail. Although Baird's sandpipers occasionally stop to rest and feed on shallow lakes within the Canadian Rockies, they nest in the Arctic. They are most often seen along the eastern slopes during their fall migration to Chile.

Pectoral Sandpiper (22 cm)
Calidris melanotos

BJKCLWY
SANDPIPER FAMILY

The pectoral is a medium-sized sandpiper with a distinct, broad, buffy breast band that is heavily and evenly streaked with fine brown lines. That band is clearly defined against a white throat and underparts. This brownish gray sandpiper is similar in color to the least and semipalmated sandpipers, but it is nearly twice as large. It is most likely to be confused with Baird's, but its crown and face are browner and it has yellow rather than black legs. The pectoral's slightly decurved bill is greenish yellow at the base becoming black at the tip. During migration, pectorals favor wet grassy areas for feeding rather than open mud flats as preferred by Baird's, least, and semipalmated sandpipers. Pectoral sandpipers breed in the arctic and subarctic tundra and occasionally migrate, particularly in the autumn, along the eastern slope of the Rockies; they are rare elsewhere in these mountains.

Least Sandpiper

Baird's Sandpiper

Pectoral Sandpiper

59

Stilt Sandpiper (22 cm)

JY

Calidris himantopus

SANDPIPER FAMILY

Stilt sandpipers are slim-bodied, long-necked, and long-legged, with a longish bill that is usually slightly depressed along the outer one-third. In breeding plumage the birds have striped crowns, chestnut stripes on the side of the head, and heavily barred underparts. In autumn plumage the underparts are not barred and the ear coverts and nape are no longer tinged with chestnut. Members of a flock generally stay close together while feeding in shallow water at the edges of pools, sloughs, and lakes. They stand as deep in the water as their long legs will permit and often plunge their whole head and neck under water in order to probe for food. Stilt sandpipers could be confused with lesser yellowlegs except for the light line over the eye and dull yellowish green legs. The latter have bright yellow legs and make frequent bobbing motions. Stilt sandpipers do not bob. They are fairly common from Jasper northward during the fall migration.

Long-billed Dowitcher (25 cm)

BJL

Limnodromus scolopaceus

SANDPIPER FAMILY

Most upperparts of the long-billed dowitcher are dark brown with the feathers edged in various shades of red, except for a large white patch on the back that is covered by the wings when at rest. The lower back and tail are barred with black and white. In flight both the white back patch and the barred tail are good field marks in any season. In breeding plumage all underparts are brick red with brownish black bars on the breast, flank, and sides and with dense brownish black spotting restricted to the upper breast and throat. A very similar species, the short-billed dowitcher *(Limnodromus griseus),* does not have well-formed bars on the sides of the breast, and the upperparts and belly are lighter in color. Both species have long, straight bills. As their common names suggest, there is generally a difference in bill length, but there is considerable overlap. The alarm call of the long-billed dowitcher is a shrill *"keek"* contrasted with the short-billed dowitcher's double or triple *"tu."* During the late summer and autumn the long-billed dowitcher is scarce on mud flats in the central and northern parts of the Rockies and rare in the south. The short-billed dowitcher is a rare spring transient in the Banff and Yoho national parks region and is slightly more abundant during the autumn.

Common Snipe (23 cm)

BJKCKLWY

Gallinago gallinago

SANDPIPER FAMILY

The common snipe is a medium-sized, brownish sandpiper with short legs, short neck, and a straight, very long bill. It has a distinctive striped head and back with a rusty tail. Except for the white belly, both the upper and underparts are boldly patterned. This snipe is fairly solitary and secretive, relying on its protective coloration to blend with the surroundings for security. When flushed a bird may rise almost at your feet with an irregular, twisty flight and a grating *"scaipe"* note of alarm, likely giving the intruder a bad fright. Common snipe breed throughout the Canadian Rockies, but are more common in the central and northern areas.

Stilt Sandpiper

Long-billed Dowitcher

Common Snipe

Wilson's Phalarope (20 cm)

BJKCKWY

Phalaropus tricolor

SANDPIPER FAMILY

There are notable reversals of sex roles exhibited by the Wilson's phalarope. The female has the more brightly colored plumage. Her breeding plumage includes a gray crown fading to white on the nape and a broad black stripe running through the eye and down the side of the neck. This stripe blends into cinnamon on the lower neck and across the upper breast. The wings are long and a uniform brownish gray. A white rump patch and whitish tail are visible in flight. Males are duller in color and smaller in size. The females are the aggressors while carrying on the courtship. When mating is completed the male is left to build the nest, incubate the eggs, and care for the young. When feeding in water a phalarope rotates like a top, stirring the bottom mud and bringing insect larvae to the surface where they collect toward the center of the miniature "whirlpool." These birds are scarce in the Canadian Rockies.

Red-necked Phalarope (15 cm)

BJKCKLY

Phalaropus lobatus

SANDPIPER FAMILY

The red-necked phalarope is smaller in size than the Wilson's. It has a red neck, a white throat patch, and the solid gray of the head and face extends almost across the breast. It lacks the neck stripes associated with the Wilson's phalarope. Both sexes have dark backs with bright buff stripes along the sides. As with other phalaropes, the breeding female is more brightly colored than the male. In flight white wing stripes, whitish stripes on the back, and dark central tail coverts are visible. The white wing bar is distinctive and will separate it in any plumage from the Wilson's. Their thin, black bill is about the same length as the head. This species' flight is darting and erratic. They use a whirligig, spin-around action in the water to stir up larvae for their next meal. The red-necked phalarope nests in the arctic and subarctic regions and winters on the oceans off both coasts. It is a scarce spring and autumn visitor to the Canadian Rockies and is rarely seen in the more southerly portion.

Franklin's Gull (35 cm)

BJKCW

Larus pipixcan

GULL FAMILY

Swirling flocks of Franklin's gulls often descend on freshly worked fields in the spring to forage for cutworms, wireworms, and a myriad of insect grubs and larvae scurrying to new shelters after the upheaval of their homes. In breeding plumage the birds have black hoods, white underparts with a variable rosy tinge, and white and black wing bars that separate the white wing tip from the slate gray wing. Conspicuous white eye crescents, almost gogglelike, contrast with the black head. Both the bill and legs are dark red. The blackness of the wings of Franklin's gulls, without prominent white wrists, is the best field mark for all plumages. The common name of this bird was given in honor of Sir John Franklin, an English explorer of the Arctic. Sizable flocks are occasionally seen along the eastern slopes of the Rockies, particularly in the extreme south. Such birds are probably transient nonbreeders.

Wilson's Phalarope

Red-necked Phalarope

Franklin's Gull

Bonaparte's Gull (28 cm)

Larus philadelphia

BJKCKLWY

GULL FAMILY

In its spring breeding plumage the Bonaparte's, like the Franklin's gull, has a black head with white eye crescents. In flight the Bonaparte's gull has prominent white wing wrists with narrow black wing tips. In contrast, the Franklin's lack the white wing wrists and have white wing tips. The bill of the Bonaparte's is black compared with the red bill of the Franklin's gull. Bonaparte's gulls nest in coniferous trees within the boreal forest. This gull was named after Charles Bonaparte, a French zoologist, not the famous general. They are occasional migrants in the central and northern areas of the Rockies; rare in the south. They likely breed in the extreme northern part but that has not been confirmed.

Mew Gull (35 cm)

Larus canus

BJLY

GULL FAMILY

The white-headed gulls, such as the mew, offer a real challenge in field identification. Adult females and males have very similar plumage but that of immature birds is highly variable. In addition to the white head, the mature mew gull has a grayish blue mantle over the back and wings with black tips on the primaries. The outermost two primaries have a large white spot on the black wing tip. Their bill is small, yellow or greenish yellow, and unmarked with spots or rings. They have large dark eyes and yellowish green legs. The mew gull may nest in colonies or as pairs. Nests are usually on the ground, but trees are used occasionally. They are a very noisy gull, repeating their *"mew"* call almost nonstop. This gull is common in the northern Rockies, occasional in the central portion, and rare in the south.

Ring-billed Gull (40 cm)

Larus delawarensis

BJKCKWY

GULL FAMILY

The ring-billed is smaller than the California gull and decidedly smaller than the herring gull. Breeding adults have a pale gray mantle over the back and wings. The black primaries of the wings are tipped with white spots. Size, however, is only a useful characteristic for field identification when mixed flocks of gulls are present at a dump or other attractive feeding or resting areas. In addition, adult ring-bills have a yellow bill with a black ring near the tip, pale yellow eyes, and yellowish legs and feet. In contrast, California gulls have red or red and black spots on the bill, but lack the black ring. Herring gulls have red on the bill, pink legs and feet, and a more angular head. Although they are not known to nest in the Canadian Rockies, the ring-billed gull is a common visitor, especially at garbage dumps, from late April to late October. Their numbers generally increase during the autumn.

Bonaparte's Gull

Mew Gull

Ring-billed Gull

California Gull (43 cm)
Larus californicus

The California gull is the state bird of Utah. It won this honor by devouring black crickets that were invading and destroying the Mormons' crops in 1848. It is an opportunist that allows few sources of food to go to waste. The California gull has a white head, body, and tail with gray upperwings and mantle. The wing tips are black with white at the outer extremities; the amount of black gradually decreases from the first to sixth primary. The bill is yellow with a red spot or red and black spots on the lower mandible and a dark spot on the upper mandible. The best combination of field marks includes the size and markings of the bill, leg color, and dark eyes. Their legs and feet are a greenish color. This gull is common around lakes, rivers, and garbage dumps in the montane zone of the Canadian Rockies. They are most numerous during August and September.

Herring Gull (50 cm)
Larus argentatus

Herring gulls are casual visitors to the Rockies as they cross the mountains between their wintering grounds on the west coast and their summer range in the boreal forest. Adult herring gulls are large with a pearl gray mantle on the back and wings. The black-tipped primaries have white spots on the two outer feathers. The remainder of the plumage is white. They have flesh pink legs and feet, pale yellow eyes, and a red spot near the tip of the lower yellow mandible. Herring gulls are great wanderers and useful scavengers, helping to keep our environment clean. They are early spring and late summer/early autumn visitors to the central and northern parts of our region.

Common Tern (35 cm)
Sterna hirundo

Common terns are often seen patrolling gracefully over large lakes in the prairie, hovering for an instant on rapidly beating wings while searching for a fish and then plummeting beneath the water surface to reappear with a squirming meal. Breeding birds have a black cap and nape with a bluish gray mantle over the back and wings. They have orange-red legs and feet and a similar-colored bill that may also be black tipped. The forked tail is about 8 cm long with a black edge on the outermost feathers. The tail does not extend beyond the folded wings. The upperwings have a dark trailing edge. The dark wing and tail markings can be used to separate the common tern from the Forster's, which occasionally visits the Rockies. The drawn out *"kee-ar"* call of the common tern can also be used to distinguish it from the *"tzaap"* call of the Forster's. The common tern is an occasional spring and fall visitor to the Rockies.

California Gull (with young)

Herring Gull

Common Tern

Black Tern (23 cm)

Chlidonias niger

BJKCWY

GULL FAMILY

The black tern is characterized as an "aquatic swallow" by some because of its ability to swoop gracefully back and forth over lakes snapping damsel flies and other insects from the air. It can also be observed diving headlong into water for some favorite tidbit. Unlike the common tern, they rarely catch fish. This small, dark tern with a fairly short, slightly notched tail is distinctive. The dark slate gray of the back and wings deepens to a dull black on the bill, head, neck, and body except for the gray rump and white undertail coverts. The underwings are a uniform pale gray. These birds nest in grassy marshes, often on floating mats of vegetation and sometimes on muskrat houses. They vigorously defend their nest site by vociferously scolding and dive-bombing intruders. The black tern is generally an occasional visitor to the Canadian Rockies, but it does breed in the Waterton region.

Rock Dove (28 cm)

Columba livia

BJKCKWY

DOVE FAMILY

Introduced from Europe, the rock dove, or pigeon, is now well established in North America. The ancestral wild type is blue-gray, darkest on the head and neck, with two black bars on the secondaries, a white rump, and dark tail tip. There is often some iridescence on the sides of the neck. Pigeon fanciers have produced an incredible number of variants. In color, the original blue-gray bird may now be white to brown or red to black with various mottlings and streaks. Feral flocks of rock doves are established in most settled areas within the Rockies and are year-round residents. Their flimsy nests consist of little more than a few stems of coarse grass and a twig or two, often on ledges of buildings or under bridges. Only two glossy white eggs are laid and the young produced are fed a thick mucus secreted from the adults' crop for the first few days. Their muffled *"coo-crooo"* sound is known to most bird lovers.

Mourning Dove (27 cm)

Zenaida macroura

BJKCKLWY

DOVE FAMILY

Its slow, mournful *"oh-woe-woe-woe"* cooing has given rise to the name of the mourning dove. The male, in particular, uses that call during the spring courtship. The display flight by the male includes a steep, towering climb which terminates in a series of graceful arcs on stiffly outspread wings. After courting, a loose nest is built in a coniferous or deciduous tree by the female from twigs supplied by the male. Generally, only two pure white eggs are laid. The young are fed first on "pigeon milk" secreted from the crop of either adult. Their wingbeats make a considerable fluttering whistle noise as the bird takes flight. The sexes are similar in appearance with gray-brown upperparts and dark gray-brown wings, including a few large blackish spots. The underparts are gray with a pinkish wash. There is a purple iridescence on the sides of the neck and a blackish spot on the side of the head. In flight the white tips on the shorter outer feathers can be seen on the long, tapered tail. Although rather scarce, mourning doves breed in the Rockies from Jasper south; they are rare north of Jasper.

G. BEYERSBERGEN

Black Tern

Rock Dove

T. ULRICH

Mourning Dove

Great Horned Owl (50 cm)

BJKCKLWY

Bubo virginianus

OWL FAMILY

The great horned owl, the provincial bird of Alberta, is powerful and aggressive. It is one of the largest owls in the Rockies and has ear tufts or horns, which are toward the sides of the head. This bird has a conspicuous white throat, finely barred stomach and is a mottled gray-brown on the back. The eyeball of the great horned owl is as large as a human eye and like other owls it has binocular vision. The enlarged cornea allows the eye to gather all available light. Its ear openings are of unequal size which helps it locate prey by sound as well as sight. The finely toothed edges of the outer primaries allow almost noiseless flights by this large predator. It also has long, sharp talons. These special adaptations make this mostly nocturnal owl an extremely effective predator on small rodents, birds, hares, and even skunks. As is the general case with owls, the female is considerably larger than the male. The call of this owl is a series of three to eight deep, soft *"hoo"* notes. They are year-round residents in the Rockies and very early nesters, sometimes incubating eggs beneath a blanket of snow.

Northern Hawk-Owl (35 cm)

BJKCKLY

Surnia ulula

OWL FAMILY

The large head, soft feathers, and large yellow eyes mark the northern hawk-owl as a true owl, but its long tail and trim lines give it a hawklike appearance. It has a black-bordered facial disk and a black patch under the yellow bill. The underpart is grayish brown with heavy barring from the breast to the underside of the tail; the upperpart is dark brown spotted with white. Northern hawk-owls are diurnal and are often seen perched conspicuously on exposed branches from which they have a commanding view for hunting. They nest in natural cavities of trees, large woodpecker holes, and in old nests of other birds such as crows. This bird is particularly fond of old burn and spruce-bog habitats. Northern hawk-owls are fairly common year-round residents in the northern foothills, scarce in the central portion, and rare in the south.

Northern Pygmy-Owl (15 cm)

BJKCKWY

Glaucidium gnoma

OWL FAMILY

This bluebird-sized owl is the smallest in our area. The northern pygmy-owl is active during daylight hours, especially near dawn and dusk. This owl is recognized by its size, long tail with several white crossbars, and two black nape patches that are outlined in white. The upperparts may be gray-brown or rusty brown; underparts are white with dark streaks. The crown and nape of this yellow-eyed owl are spotted as are the back and wings but to a lesser extent. There is a brownish bar across the whitish part of the lower throat. Calls of the northern pygmy-owl are a low *"hoo"* repeated several times. Rodents and birds make up a substantial part of its diet, and it sometimes catches prey larger than itself. Tree cavities and old woodpecker holes are favorite nesting sites. This owl is an uncommon year-round resident. It is scarce in the northern area.

E. JONES

Great Horned Owl

Northern Hawk-Owl

J. WASSINK

Northern Pygmy-Owl

71

Barred Owl (43 cm)

Strix varia

BJKCKLWY

OWL FAMILY

Some birders claim the most frequent sound from the barred owl is a nine-noted *"who-cooks-for-you, who-cooks-for-you-all?"* These words at least give the rhythm of the call if not the intent. This owl is a large, big-headed bird without ear tufts. The upperparts are grayish brown and heavily barred with buffy white on the head, neck, tail, and wings. Underparts are whitish with a combination of dark bars on the breast and dark stripes on the abdomen. This owl's facial disk is accented by two obsidian black eyes. The barred owl has large ear openings slightly different in size and shape that help in determining the exact location of the faintest sound, which is important to this strictly nocturnal hunter. Its diet consists largely of small mammals of the night. Barred owls are occasional year-round residents throughout the Canadian Rockies. They nest in the hollows of trees or in the unused nests of large birds.

Great Gray Owl (55 cm)

Strix nebulosa

BJKCKLWY

OWL FAMILY

The head of the great gray owl looks almost too large to be supported by its body. The prominent concentric circles on facial disks and the large bright yellow eyes emphasize the head size. Its big head, long tail, and thick coat of fluffy feathers make this owl appear larger than it really is. The gray-toned plumage is marked with longitudinal streaks on the crown and neck. A white "bow tie" on the throat is a distinctive field mark. Most often seen hunting toward dusk, the great gray silently swoops down from conspicuous perches on unsuspecting prey. Although efficient mousers, they also take hares, squirrels, and small birds. A year-round resident, the great gray uses abandoned nests of hawks or crows for rearing its young. It is more frequent in the north than the south, but it is never abundant.

Long-eared Owl (37 cm)

Asio otus

BY

OWL FAMILY

This crow-sized owl has obvious, long ear tufts that are close-set toward the middle of the head. The facial disk of the long-eared owl ranges from a typical orange-chestnut to a tawny brown. Its breast is dark brownish gray with irregular white spots. The belly and sides are white, boldly striped, and crosshatched with brown. Upperparts are dark brown mottled with grayish white. The wings of the long-eared owl extend beyond the tail. Its flight is buoyant and erratic. When disturbed by intruders, these owls frequently give a threat display by spreading their wings. They sally forth at night to hunt, carrying death and destruction into the ranks of small nocturnal rodents such as mice and shrews. Long-eared owls raise their brood in a nest once built by a crow, magpie, or hawk. Although they are known to breed in the montane zone of Banff National Park, they are rare in the Canadian Rockies.

Great Gray Owl

Barred Owl

Long-eared Owl

Boreal Owl (25 cm)

Aegolius funereus

BJKCKLY

OWL FAMILY

The boreal owl has a whitish facial disk with a distinct outer black border. Its upperparts are chocolate brown thickly spotted with white on the forehead, crown, and around the facial disk and only occasionally spotted on the shoulders and wings. The white spots on the forehead, yellow bill, and larger size are field marks that separate it from the northern saw-whet owl. While lethargic by day, this skillful hunter gobbles up bats, mice, shrews, and voles during the night. Boreal owls are scarce year-round residents, nesting in natural cavities of trees or large woodpecker holes in the central and northern parts of the Rockies. They are rarely seen in the south.

Northern Saw-whet Owl (18 cm)

Aegolius acadicus

BJKCK

OWL FAMILY

The black bill, white streaks instead of spots on the forehead, and smaller size distinguish the northern saw-whet owl from the boreal owl. This owl is reddish brown above and has reddish facial disks without a dark border. The upperparts are white with broad streaks of reddish brown on the breast and sides. This tiny owl has large, lemon yellow eyes. Although rather difficult to find, the saw-whet is exceedingly tame and can be approached to close range. Sometimes it can actually be caught in the hands. Their calls include a series of *"too-too-too-too."* The saw-whetting call, from which it takes its common name, is said to resemble the sound made by filing or whetting a saw. That call is seldom given. This diminutive owl passes the day perched motionless close to the trunk of a tree blending indistinguishably with the bark. An active hunter during the night, the saw-whet's diet consists mainly of insects and mice. It is an occasional year-round resident in the central and southern regions, generally depending on woodpecker holes for nesting sites.

Common Nighthawk (23 cm)

Chordeiles minor

BJKCKLWY

GOATSUCKER FAMILY

Common nighthawks have extremely small bills and enormous mouths that are used to catch airborne insects which are taken on the wing. Their upperparts are blackish, mottled with whites, buffs, and browns. The underparts are white with heavy blackish gray bars. Conspicuous field markings include a frosty white throat patch and a bar across the wings midway between the bend and the tip. Males have a white band on the tail. Females lack the white tail band and the throat and wing patches may be a buffy white. Common nighthawks are marvelously adapted to aerial acrobatics having long, pointed, falcon-shaped wings. During courtship, the male nighthawk produces an unusual booming sound with its wings as it pulls up at the end of a spectacular aerial dive. Their flights while hunting the sky for flying insects are erratic and often accompanied at frequent intervals by a *"peent"* call. Nighthawks are an occasional bird in the Rockies, nesting on the ground in open places.

Boreal Owl

A. NELSON

Northern Saw-whet Owl

T. ULRICH

Common Nighthawk

Black Swift (18 cm)

BJKCKWY

Cypseloides niger

SWIFT FAMILY

Both sexes of black swifts are usually a uniform sooty black but some individuals have white edgings on the feathers of the forehead, belly, and undertail coverts. In flight the front edges of the very long, narrow wings form a swept-back arc. Their slightly forked tail is usually spread during flight. Their flight is characterized by rapid, even wingbeats alternating with long, sweeping sails. They forage high in the air and considerable distances from the nesting sites, which are often on the walls of mountain canyons near waterfalls. Black swifts lay only one egg which hatches in late July. Breeding may be delayed so that hatching will coincide with the flight of flying ants. Preliminary information suggests that the diet of black swifts after the hatching of their young is predominantly flying ants. Baby swifts, fed infrequently by regurgitation, can survive unattended for several days by going into torpor. There are nesting colonies of black swifts at Johnston's Canyon in Banff and Maligne Canyon in Jasper.

Vaux's Swift (11 cm)

KWY

Chaetura vauxi

SWIFT FAMILY

The Vaux's swift is dark brown above and a slightly lighter gray-brown below, particularly on the throat and breast. Its body is slim and cigar-shaped with a short, stubby tail. Each tail feather ends with a short spine. This swift often nests on the broken tops of western red cedar, gluing nest material together with saliva produced by seasonally enlarged salivary glands. They forage for insects in the air at various heights and over many different habitats. Their distribution is restricted largely to old-growth stands in the Columbian forest on the western slope of the Canadian Rockies where they are seen occasionally.

Black Swift (feeding young)

Black Swift (immature)

Vaux's Swift

Calliope Hummingbird (7 cm)

BJKCKWY

Stellula calliope

There are five kinds of hummingbirds in the Canadian Rockies. One of these, the calliope, is the smallest bird in North America, weighing about 25 g. The male has purple-red streaked feathers, or gorget as it is called, on a white throat. They are the best field marks in good light. The rays of the gorget are more elongated toward the sides of the throat. This hummer is generally iridescent green above and white below. Females are bronze-green above with a tinge of buff on the underparts, flanks, and at the base of the tail. They lack the gorget rays, but their throats are finely freckled with dark colors. Their tails are black toward the end with white tips on the outer feathers. Both sexes have a relatively short, straight bill and a short, broad, unforked tail. Females and young are so similar to those of the rufous hummingbird that they cannot be distinguished in the field with any certainty. During courtship the male swoops back and forth exhibiting his brilliantly colored gorget and defending his territory with great vigor. These outrageously aggressive birds do not hesitate to dive-bomb birds much larger than themselves. Often located on pine boughs, the tiny cup-shaped nests are made from plant down, mosses, and lichens and bound together with spider webs. Only two bean-sized, white eggs are laid. The male loses interest once the eggs are laid and soon departs. The female feeds the young a fluid food from her crop. Like other hummers, its primary food is nectar and tiny insects collected from flowers as it zooms from plant to plant. They feed so actively that their bills, forehead, and chin are often discolored by pollen. This hummer has a particular preference for red flowers. In flight their wings beat so fast, 55 to 75 times per second, that they appear as a blur and cause a distinct humming sound. In the bird world, hummingbirds alone are capable of backward flight. The calliope hummingbird is primarily a western species and occurs in Alberta only along the Canadian Rockies from Jasper south.

Calliope Hummingbird (female)

Calliope Hummingbird (male)

T. ULRICH

Calliope Hummingbird (male)

T. ULRICH

Rufous Hummingbird (9 cm)

Selasphorus rufus

BJKCKLWY

HUMMINGBIRD FAMILY

The rufous hummingbird is the most common and widely distributed of the hummers in the Canadian Rockies. The cinnamon red male has a shiny green patch on top of the head and a scarlet gorget that sometimes appears black. The female is green above and has reddish brown areas on the flanks and tail and small red to green spots on the throat. In the spring, a male zealously defends his feeding and nesting territory in a very pugnacious manner. His courtship display is a series of dives and rising loops in an oval pattern, with swoops just inches from the female while displaying his brilliant gorget. After a pair mate, the male takes no part in the affairs of the family. The female builds the nest within the protective branches of an evergreen tree with bits of lichen on the outside wall to give it the appearance of a natural knob. The young are blind and almost naked on hatching. The mother broods them and feeds them regurgitated food from her bill. She also picks up the droppings and carries them away. The principal food of adult birds consists of nectar from brightly colored flowers and insects caught on the wing. They are easily attracted to feeders containing a sugar solution. A remarkable feature of hummingbirds is their flight, a true marvel of nature. They may stop, go backward, then forward, hover, and then dart off at incredible speeds. The rapid wing motion produces a hum which has given rise to the bird's name. The rufous hummingbird is fairly common in any habitat from the montane to alpine zones, where meadows of wildflowers are available. Although it is our most northerly hummingbird, the rufous is more abundant from Jasper south.

Rufous Hummingbird (male)

Rufous Hummingbird (female)

Rufous Hummingbird (at nest)

Belted Kingfisher (30 cm)

Ceryle alcyon

Belted kingfishers are fairly common residents along fish-inhabited waterways throughout the Canadian Rockies. It is called a belted kingfisher because of the blue-gray band across the breast of the male, with an additional reddish band below the blue-gray one on females. The belted kingfisher is blue-gray above and mostly white below. Also noticeable are the big, unruly crest and large, sharp bill. It has a distinctive, loud rattling call both in flight and while perched. There are small white spots near the eyes and on the upper side of the wings and tail. The bird's flight pattern, a series of five or six wingbeats alternating with long glides, is a distinctive characteristic. Kingfishers nest in holes dug in steep earth banks.

Lewis' Woodpecker (23 cm)

Melanerpes lewis

The Lewis' woodpecker has a greenish black back, wings, and tail with deep red at the base of the bill and under the eyes. It has a silvery gray breast that extends as a narrow band around the back of the neck. The pinkish red lower breast and belly distinguishes the Lewis' from all other species of woodpecker. This woodpecker has some peculiar habits. It eats fruits and is a master at catching insects on the wing. Unlike most woodpeckers, it chooses to perch on the top of fenceposts or tree stumps rather than clinging to the bark of trees. In addition it has a slow, steady flight pattern like that of a crow. The Lewis' woodpecker prefers open country with large trees such as ponderosa pine. They nest in an excavated tree cavity, most typically in a dead tree. This woodpecker is rare along the eastern slopes of the Rockies and occasional on the western slope in open brushy and burned-over areas. It has nested from Jasper south.

Yellow-bellied Sapsucker (20 cm)

Sphyrapicus varius

The male yellow-bellied sapsucker can be identified by a distinctive white wing bar, a mottled black-and-white back, a red forehead and throat, and a black chest band above the yellowish belly. Females are similar to the adult males except the throat is generally white instead of red and the amount of red on the crown may be reduced or replaced by black. Yellow-bellied sapsuckers prefer aspen, birch, or poplar trees for drilling regularly spaced holes in horizontal lines. These holes, drilled at a slightly upward angle, act as miniature reservoirs to collect the exuded sap. True to its name, this bird has a special brush on the end of its tongue for lapping up the sap which has oozed into the holes as well as small insects attracted to it. Nesting occurs in a hole they excavate in a tree. Yellow-bellied sapsuckers are uncommon in deciduous forests in the central and northern regions and rare in the southern region. Red-naped sapsuckers *(Sphyrapicus nuchalis)* are very similar except that both sexes have a red patch on the back of the crown and adult females have red at least on the lower throat. They are uncommon from Jasper southward.

Belted Kingfisher

Lewis' Woodpecker

Yellow-bellied Sapsucker

83

Downy Woodpecker (15 cm)
Picoides pubescens

The downy woodpecker is the smallest and one of the most widely distributed of North American woodpeckers. They are black and white with a broad white stripe down their back from the shoulders to the rump. Their wings are checkered in a black-and-white pattern which shows through on the wings' undersides. Their breasts and flanks are white. The crowns of their heads are black and their neck and cheeks are adorned by black and white lines. The males have a small scarlet patch, like a pompom, at the back of the crown. The downy's outer tail feathers are barred with black. Its bill is shorter than its head and is used mainly for prying small flakes of bark from the tree as they search for insects. Downys feed on a myriad of small larvae and insects hidden under the bark. With short legs and two toes that point forward and two backward on each foot, the downy has an excellent grip for climbing. It climbs by using its stiff, sharply pointed tail feathers as a prop while shifting its leghold. This woodpecker is a year-round resident, occasionally seen in aspen and poplar groves during the spring and summer, but seen less frequently during the winter.

Hairy Woodpecker (20 cm)
Picoides villosus

The hairy is an enlarged model of the downy woodpecker, being 5 to 8 cm longer than its smaller cousin. The best distinction is the hairy's bill which is as long as its head, while that of the downy is obviously shorter than the head. Another major difference is that the outer tail feathers are white, instead of being barred with black. This woodpecker has a barbed, lancelike tongue that can be thrust out a great distance. Once a hole is drilled, the tongue is injected to pierce wood-boring insects or larvae, then quickly pulled back into the bill. The loud drumming sound and sharp *"peek"* call often draw attention to the hairy woodpecker. During courtship, both sexes will drum long, rolling tattoos on a dead tree. Then they take off in a courtship flight with the wings beating against the flanks to produce sound. A nest cavity is excavated in a dead or dying aspen, and takes seven to twenty-one days to complete. It is an occasional year-round resident throughout the Rockies.

Three-toed Woodpecker (20 cm)
Picoides tridactylus

The three-toed woodpecker is one of two species of woodpeckers with three, instead of four, toes. Black and white bars, or a longitudinal white stripe, down the center of the back of the three-toed distinguish it from the similar black-backed woodpecker. Both species have heavily barred sides and both males have a yellow cap. The female three-toed lacks the yellow cap and, except for her barred sides, resembles the hairy woodpecker. This woodpecker prefers coniferous forests and is especially attracted to newly and severely burned-over areas. Wood-burrowing insects are the common source of food. A year-round resident, the three-toed is more common in subalpine forests from Jasper to the north. It is less abundant on the eastern slopes south of Banff.

Hairy Woodpecker (male)

Downy Woodpecker (male)

Three-toed Woodpecker (male)

Black-backed Woodpecker (21 cm)
Picoides arcticus

The black-backed is the only woodpecker with a white breast and throat and solidly black back. They have heavily barred sides like the three-toed and males have a similar yellow cap. Females are lighter-colored, shorter-billed, and lack the yellow cap. The black-backed is much more aggressive and vocally active than the very similar hairy woodpecker with which it shares the coniferous forests. Black-backed woodpeckers forage on dead conifers, flaking away large patches of loose bark in search of insects and larvae of wood-boring beetles. They prefer burnt areas where dead stumps and decaying trees provide both food and nesting sites. This woodpecker is scarce from Jasper south and is occasional from Jasper north.

Northern Flicker (27 cm)
Colaptes auratus

In the past, two species of flickers were recognized in the Canadian Rockies, the red-shafted and the yellow-shafted. They are now designated as one species, the northern flicker, with two subspecies. The subspecies differ by color markings on the feather shafts and adjacent areas. Since they freely interbreed with each other there are many hybrid characteristics. All races of this flicker have barred black and brown backs with a white rump patch that is visible during the undulating flights. Underparts of all are buffy white with black spots and have a broad black bib. The underwings and tail vary from a rich salmon red to a brilliant golden yellow. Some races have a gray crown, red nape patch, and black mustache; others have a brown crown and a gray face with a red mustache. Females lack the mustache stripe. Each foot has two toes pointed forward and two pointed rearward, an adaptation for a successful life on tree trunks. Although often seen in trees, they spend much time feeding on the ground. Ants make up the majority of their diet. Their tongue, which can be extended more than 5 cm, is coated with sticky saliva designed for catching those insects. Flickers are noisy with a variety of calls, including the harsh *"wick-er"* cry. The flicker is the carpenter of the bird world, using its chisel-like bill to excavate a new nesting cavity each year. Many other cavity-nesting species, such as American kestrels and northern saw-whet owls, which are unable to do their own excavating, rely on flickers to supply them with nesting quarters. Flickers are a common bird of the forests throughout the Canadian Rockies.

Black-backed Woodpecker (male)

Northern Flicker (male, red-shafted race)

Northern Flicker (female, red-shafted race)

Northern Flicker (male, yellow-shafted race)

Pileated Woodpecker (38 cm)
Dryocopus pileatus

BJKCKLWY
WOODPECKER FAMILY

The crow-sized pileated (pronounced PILE-e-a-ted) is the largest woodpecker in the Canadian Rockies. Its species name, *pileatus,* means crested, a reference to the prominent bright red crest which extends back from the forehead over the crown. In females the red is confined to the crest. No other woodpecker in our area is crested. Both sexes are black-bodied with broad white underwings that are conspicuous in flight. They also have a white chin and dark bill. The sexes can also be distinguished by the male's mustache which is red at its start near his lower bill compared with an entirely black mustache on females. This woodpecker is a master avian tree surgeon, using its powerful bill to chisel out rectangular or triangular holes in standing dead trees. Several of these large cavities are used for roosting and a similar one is used for nesting. It visits rotten logs and tears and scatters them about while looking for the grubs contained inside. It also drills into carpenter ant galleries and quickly removes them with its long, sticky tongue. Other characteristics of this bird include a heavy undulating flight and a wide range of loud calls. Although scarce and localized in distribution, the pileated is a year-round resident in the montane forests of our area. It prefers Douglas fir mixed forests as a habitat.

Olive-sided Flycatcher (16 cm)
Contopus borealis

BJKCKLWY
FLYCATCHER FAMILY

The olive-sided flycatcher has a dark grayish olive mantle and no eye-ring. It has two distinctive features. First, the brownish olive flanks and sides are separated by a white or pale yellow throat, center breast, and belly. Second, small white tufts on the back are clearly visible in flight but may be covered by the wings when the bird is at rest. Their call notes include a loud, penetrating *"quick-THREE beeeer"* and a lower-pitched *"pep-pep-pep."* The olive-sided is easily seen since it often chooses to perch on the tip of a dead branch before darting off to another high, conspicuous twig. They are a common breeding bird in the coniferous forests of the Rockies. Burned-over areas with standing dead trees and open forests are among their preferred habitats.

Western Wood-Pewee (13 cm)
Contopus sordidulus

BJKCKWY
FLYCATCHER FAMILY

This small flycatcher is grayish olive above and has whitish underparts with an olive-gray wash on the sides of the breast. Two faint whitish wing bars are present on adult birds; first-winter birds have buff wing bars. They have no conspicuous eye-rings. Calls of the western wood-pewee include a harsh nasal *"peeer"* that is slightly descending. That penetrating call may be repeated and repeated throughout the day. The western wood-pewee is almost exclusively an insect-eater. It is an occasional breeding bird in the montane zone, particularly in damper areas.

E. JONES

Pileated Woodpecker

Olive-sided Flycatcher

T. ULRICH

Western Wood-Pewee

Willow Flycatcher (13 cm)
Empidonax traillii

Typical willow flycatchers are olive to brownish olive on the back with a white throat and white abdomen that is washed a light sulphur color toward the vent. It has buff-white wing bars and an ill-defined eye-ring. Willow and alder *(Empidonax alnorum)* flycatchers are so similar and overlapping in characteristics that identification is not certain even in the hand. These birds are best identified by voice. The willow has a sneezy *"fitz-bew"* song with both syllables equally accented. The alder's song is a raspy *"fee-BEE-o."* They both frequent willow and alder thickets, usually along streams. These flycatchers are quite shy and flit away from inquisitive observers. The alder is a fairly common flycatcher in the montane zone from Jasper northward. In contrast, the willow flycatcher is more common in the montane zone from Banff south.

Least Flycatcher (11 cm)
Empidonax minimus

The least is the smallest flycatcher in Canada. It shares the breeding habitat of the alder and willow flycatchers and resembles them very closely. The least generally has slightly gray upperparts and the underparts are more whitish, possibly with a slight yellowish tinge on the lower belly and flanks. It has white wing bars, noticeable white eye-rings and a slightly forked tail. Many people despair of identifying these flycatchers by anything except their voices. The least has an explosive *"che-BEK"* call, like a hacking cough, which can be repeated several times. They prefer open deciduous forests, especially aspen stands or mixedwoods. These avid eaters of insects are often seen flitting from perch to perch in search of their next meal. This flycatcher is common from Banff northward, rare in the extreme south, and scarce on the western slopes.

Hammond's Flycatcher (12 cm)
Empidonax hammondii

Some bird books go on ad infinitum on how to tell the Hammond's from the dusky flycatcher *(Empidonax oberholseri)*. Personally, I think that only God can tell them apart in the field and even He may have difficulty! Both species have grayish olive upperparts, pale olive gray breasts and sides, gray throats, yellowish to whitish abdomens and undertail coverts, and white eye-rings. Even their voices are very similar. The Hammond's song is usually a three-parted *"sweep-tsurp-SEEP"* while the dusky gives a *"seweep-hreek-seep"* call, sometimes with a fourth part. These sequences can be varied and syllabication may be interpreted differently by other birders. Habitat preferences are helpful in separating these species, but not infallible. The Hammond's is fond of mature coniferous forests at high elevations to near timberline. The dusky prefers willow and alder thickets and open deciduous and mixed forests in the montane zone. Both birds breed throughout most of the Canadian Rockies.

Willow Flycatcher

T. ULRICH

Least Flycatcher

A. NELSON

Hammond's Flycatcher

T. ULRICH

Western Flycatcher (13 cm)
Empidonax difficilis

The yellow throat and decidedly yellow underparts separate the western from other small flycatchers in the Rockies. Its upperparts are olive green and its wings are dark with prominent pale yellow to white wing bars and eye-rings. The dark tail has no pale edge. Their heads look large because the crown feathers may be partially erect. The lower mandible is light colored to the tip. Its variable song is often a *"pseet-ptsick-seet."* These birds appear nervous, frequently flicking their wings and tails simultaneously. This flycatcher prefers moist, shaded forests along ravines and stream courses in the montane region. It is a ground-nesting flycatcher, especially along steep stream banks. The western flycatcher is scarce throughout most of the Rockies.

Eastern Kingbird (17 cm)
Tyrannus tyrannus

The eastern kingbird is one of the few flycatchers that is easily identified. Its crown and the sides of its face are black with the other upperparts a dark bluish black except for a few wing feathers that are narrowly edged with white. Unmistakable is the black tail banded with white at the tip as if it had been dipped in white paint. It is white below with a grayish wash on the sides and upper breast. Calls include a harsh *"dzeet"* and a more prolonged *"kipper."* Eastern kingbirds are pugnacious and any bird near its home will be vigorously challenged. They attack crows, hawks, and other large birds with a persistent energy and a fearlessness that is surprising in so small a bird. After the defense of hearth and home the eastern kingbird perches in the open, waiting to dash out and catch a passing insect. They are partial to a vicinity near water and to open places. It is a fairly common breeding bird in such areas throughout the Rockies.

Horned Lark (17 cm)
Eremophila alpestris

Horned larks have several distinctive features that make them easy to identify. The face is yellow to white with a broad black stripe from the bill to under the eye that then curves downward. It also has a black band across the forehead with two tiny black "horns" that are often difficult to see except during the breeding season. This lark has a pinkish brown back and is black-tailed except for white outer tail feathers and brown central tail feathers. The underparts are buffy with a black bib across the upper chest. Females are duller overall with less prominent horns. Like other larks it has a very long hind toenail. The courtship flight of the male is spectacular. He flies upward 100 m or more, usually in full song, then dives downward in a free fall until he nears the ground. The horned lark is a bird that prefers open spaces with a minimum of ground cover. In the Canadian Rockies this lark is common in the alpine zone from Banff northward. They nest in a hollow on the ground and feed on insects, fruits, and seeds.

Western Flycatcher

Eastern Kingbird

Horned Lark

Tree Swallow (13 cm)
Tachycineta bicolor

BJKCKLWY
SWALLOW FAMILY

Tree swallows have glossy blue-black upperparts with the dark color extending well below the eye. The underparts are white. This handsome bird has a slightly forked tail. Adult females are similar to males but the upperparts are usually duller; yearling females have a brownish back. Tree swallows are the first swallows to return in the spring, hawking insects over ponds and still frozen lakes. Insects, largely caught on the wing, comprise most of this swallow's diet. Tree swallows have gaping mouths which are excellent for scooping up such winged invertebrates. They nest in tree cavities, generally over or near water. Tree swallows are easily induced to use man-made nestboxes. Their habit of feeding on bothersome insects, their beauty, and their grace of flight are ample rewards for establishing such boxes. Unlike most other swallows, the tree swallow is not colonial. They are a common breeding bird throughout our area.

Violet-green Swallow (12 cm)
Tachycineta thalassina

BJKCKLWY
SWALLOW FAMILY

Closely resembling a tree swallow, the violet-green adult male has a rich velvety green back with a wash of purple or violet on the crown, rump, uppertail coverts, and wing coverts. The white underpart extends to above the eyes in contrast to tree swallows where the white is well below the eyes. In flight it displays two prominent white patches on either side of the rump and a notched tail. Adult females are much duller and often brownish on the crown and nape. These birds forage above open water, over forest tops, and at great heights above the ground. They nest in tree cavities and crevices on mountain cliffs and readily take to nestboxes. The violet-green swallow is common throughout the Canadian Rockies. Summer visitors to Lake Louise can generally see these birds twisting and turning in flight as they hawk for insects over the water.

Northern Rough-winged Swallow (12 cm)
Stelgidopteryx serripennis

BJKCKWY
SWALLOW FAMILY

Northern rough-winged swallows are medium brown above and whitish below with an ashy brown wash on the chin, throat, and upper breast. The name rough-winged stems from a peculiar modification of the wing. The roughness on the edge of the outer primaries results from fine, recurved hooks, barely visible to the eye but plainly perceptible to the touch. Unlike the bank swallow, the rough-winged does not nest in dense colonies but in small groups or as isolated pairs. The flight pattern of this swallow is a helpful aid in identification. Their wingbeats are deeper, slower, and more fluid than that of the bank swallow. These birds forage for insects over both water and land. They generally nest in holes in riverbanks or cliffs. Breeding from Jasper south, the northern rough-winged swallow is fairly common in our mountains.

Tree Swallow

E. JONES

Violet-green Swallow

E. JONES

Northern Rough-winged Swallow

Bank Swallow (12 cm)
Riparia riparia

Bank swallows are very gregarious and usually nest in large colonies. The burrows that they excavate with their bill and legs can be 1 m long and about 5 cm in diameter with the nesting area being larger. The tunnel slopes slightly upward from the entrance to the nesting chamber to prevent flooding. Such excavations pepper the cliffs above riverbanks and man-made banks along roadside cuts. The holes, which may be only 25 cm apart, are occupied year after year. Bank swallows are a smallish, brown-backed bird, darkest on the head and over the ear coverts, with a clearly defined grayish brown breast band on the otherwise white underparts. Their scientific name, *riparia,* means riverbank in Latin and aptly indicates the favorite habitat of bank swallows. In contrast to northern rough-winged that are quite similar in appearance, the wingbeats of bank swallows are shallow and rapid. They are a fairly common breeding bird throughout much of our area.

Cliff Swallow (13 cm)
Hirundo pyrrhonota

Cliff swallows are master masons, building their homes on cliff overhangs, under the eaves of buildings, or the underside of bridges. Both sexes of cliff swallows scoop up mud with their mouths, mix it with saliva, and plaster it pellet by pellet on some vertical surface until their gourd-shaped condominiums are clustered so close together that their sides touch. The entrances are often on the end of a short neck and pointed downward for protection from rain. Cliff swallows are chunky birds with a squarish tail and a cinnamon rump that is a good field mark. The blue-black of the upperparts is broken by narrow white stripes on the back, a pale collar across the nape, and a white to buff forehead. They are a rich chestnut on the sides of the head and throat with a small patch of black on the lower throat. Otherwise, the underparts are pale gray except for the whitish belly. These colonial nesters are tolerant of humans and are common around towns and other man-made structures throughout the Rockies.

Barn Swallow (15 cm)
Hirundo rustica

Barn swallows are easily recognized by their long, deeply-forked tails, dark steel-blue upperparts, and chestnut-colored throat. They are the only swallow in the Rockies with a deeply forked tail and with white on the tail feathers. These swallows originally nested in caves or on sheltered, rocky faces of cliffs. Now they often use man-made buildings and bridges for their nesting platform. Small pellets of mud, reinforced with straw, are built up layer by layer. The barn swallow uses its body to shape the nest that is later lined with grasses and feathers. Nests must be sheltered from rain because wetness causes them to disintegrate. These birds often nest as single pairs or in small colonies. They feed on the wing and often perch by the dozens along wires. Barn swallows are fairly common in settled areas of the Rockies.

J. WASSINK

Bank Swallow

Cliff Swallow

T. ULRICH

Barn Swallow

Gray Jay (25 cm)
Perisoreus canadensis

BJKCKLWY
CORVID FAMILY

The gray jay is a bird with a host of descriptive nicknames including whiskey-jack, camp robber, meat bird, lumberjack, moose bird, and Canada jay. This robin-sized bird is the only gray-colored jay in our area. It has a blackish head with a white forehead. The legs are black, and light gray "whiskers" surround the base of the black bill. The jay's eyes, outlined in dark gray, are a lustrous brown. Gray jays eat any kind of food including carrion, beetles, grubs, eggs, caterpillars, and scraps found at campsites and dumps. Gray jays utter a great variety of sounds. The most commonly heard is a soft, whistled *"yoo-yoo."* These birds are generally encountered singly or in pairs, often appearing silently to greet visitors and to claim their share of the lunch. The gray jay, one of the earliest nesters, is a year-round resident throughout the Canadian Rockies.

Steller's Jay (28 cm)
Cyanocitta stelleri

BJKCKLWY
CORVID FAMILY

The beautiful Steller's jay has recently been designated as the provincial bird of British Columbia. It is a true jay in all its habits being bold, greedy, and domineering along with a natural wariness. The Steller's has deep blue wings, belly, and tail with a smoky black head, breast, and back. It has black legs and bill and a conspicuous, pointed crest that is also black. The Rocky Mountain race has a white spot above each eye. These birds have an extensive vocal repertoire with the most usual call a harsh *"shaack"* which is repeated. They feed on seeds, berries, and insects and are a destructive poacher on the eggs and young of other birds. Steller's jays are resident in the Rockies throughout the year. They are fairly common in subalpine coniferous forests on the western slopes and in extreme southwestern Alberta; they are scarce from Crowsnest Pass to Jasper and rare in the north.

Blue Jay (30 cm)
Cyanocitta cristata

BJKCL
CORVID FAMILY

Blue jays are handsome, boisterous, and flamboyant. Many other adjectives could be applied, including beautiful and clever, pushy and loud, mischievous and aggressive, to clownish and saucy. Blue jays are a little larger than a robin. They are white-faced with a sky blue crest, back, wings, and tail, all strongly marked with black and white. Their underparts are whitish with a black necklace. The elongated crown feathers, or crest, are raised or lowered according to the bird's mood. In moments of aggression and high excitement the crest may be fully erect. Blue jays have an extended vocabulary with an extremely varied number of calls. Best known is the *"jay-jay-jay"* cry when the bird discovers danger nearby. Blue jays are omnivorous, eating almost anything from fruits, insects, eggs, and nestlings, to sunflower seeds and peanuts from feeders. These birds are rare in the Canadian Rockies and only found on the eastern slopes from Waterton to Jasper and in northern British Columbia. Their numbers will likely increase as more feeders become available for winter use.

Gray Jay

Steller's Jay

Blue Jay

Clark's Nutcracker (28 cm)
Nucifraga columbiana

BJKCKWY

CORVID FAMILY

The Clark's nutcracker is a symbol of the high country, breeding in a variety of high-altitude conifer habitats. It nests in coniferous trees, and its summer diet consists mainly of pine seeds, other seeds, insects, and berries. This nutcracker has a smoky gray body with black wings and central tail feathers. In flight its white wing patches and outer tail feathers are conspicuous. Clark's nutcracker was named after Captain William Clark, of the Lewis and Clark Expedition, who first brought the species to the attention of science. The nutcracker name was derived from the bird's dexterity in using its long bill in the fashion of a pick and crowbar to extract individual pine seeds from a cone. In many ways the Clark's nutcracker looks and acts like a crow. They are very noisy and talkative birds, often uttering a harsh and grating *"kra-a-a"* call. These birds are often seen begging or pilfering food at tourist stops at high elevations in the mountain parks. They are year-round residents in the south and central portions of the Rockies but are seen more often in the spring and summer.

Black-billed Magpie (45 cm)
Pica pica

BJKCKLWY

CORVID FAMILY

The scientific name *pica* means black and white, and it aptly describes the contrasting plumage of the black-billed magpie. Magpies are also distinctive because of their long, wedge-shaped tails that are an iridescent bluish green in the sunlight. Magpies are scavengers, often profiting from predator and road kills. Walking with a jerky gait or hopping on both feet, they also spend time on the ground searching for insects. Magpies also have an undulating flight pattern that makes them easily identifiable on the wing. These highly social birds are noisy, intelligent, and very wary. Typical calls include a soft *"mag,"* and a raucous *"chek."* They nest in trees or tall shrubs. Their bulky nest is a domed-over mass of sticks with one or more entrances in the sides. Magpies are year-round residents in the montane zone and may be locally common.

American Crow (43 cm)
Corvus brachyrhynchos

BJKCKLWY

CORVID FAMILY

The American crow is a large bird that is jet black all over with considerable purplish to greenish blue gloss on the back, wings, and tail. It can only be confused with the common raven, but the crow is smaller and the throat feathers blend together in a smooth mass. Crows have squared tails in contrast to the wedge-shaped tails of common ravens. The crow gives a *"caw"* call, singly or in a series, that is distinctive from that of the common raven. Crows are gregarious birds, except during the breeding season, and prefer open or semiopen habitats. They are omnivorous and will eat practically anything edible, vegetable or animal. Crows are a serious destroyer of the eggs and young of other birds. Bulky, stick nests are built in tall shrubs or in trees. Crows are common in the montane zone throughout the Rockies but, unlike ravens, do not winter here.

Clark's Nutcracker

Black-billed Magpie

American Crow

✓ Common Raven (53 cm)   BJKCKLWY
Corvus corax   CORVID FAMILY

The common raven is similar but much larger than the American crow, although size is an uncertain field guide to discern at a distance. In addition, ravens have long pointed feathers on the throat that create a shaggy appearance, a rounded or wedge-shaped tail, and a heavier bill. Their ebony plumage has a metallic sheen on the upperparts. Ravens use at least thirty distinct calls to communicate with each other. They can vocally imitate other animals, even humans. The most common call, however, is a low, drawn-out *"croak"* or *"quak."* Ravens are opportunistic feeders, eating anything from seeds, berries, insects, and carrion to refuse at landfills. Ravens are common throughout the Canadian Rockies during all times of the year, generally nesting on the face of a cliff or in a conifer.

∨ Black-capped Chickadee (11 cm)   BJKCKLWY
Parus atricapillus   CHICKADEE FAMILY

The black-capped chickadee is gray above with a white underside shading to buff along its flanks. Its black cap, drawn over the sparkling eyes, and black bib contrast with the pure white cheek patches. The wing coverts are edged in white. These hardy little birds are year-round residents. They have soft, fluffy feathers which when erected trap warm air close to the body; this serves as insulation against the cold of winter. From sunrise to sunset, the chickadee spends most of its time eating insect eggs, larvae, pupae, and other insects which are turned into energy to resist the intense cold. When food is plentiful, the chickadee may tuck morsels away for later use. The chickadee makes a variety of calls, the best known is the *"chick-a-dee-dee-dee"* that gives the bird its name. In the late winter and spring they may give a whistled *"PHEEE-bee"* or *"PHEEE-bee-bee."* During courtship the male often feeds the female. She accepts his offerings, crouching and shivering her wings like a baby bird. They often nest in a hole of a rotten stump, in a hole of a tree which they have dug out together, or in an unused woodpecker cavity. These cheerful, friendly little birds are common throughout the montane zone of the Rockies.

✓ Mountain Chickadee (11 cm)   BJKCKWY
Parus gambeli   CHICKADEE FAMILY

The mountain chickadee is similar to the black-capped except it is gray rather than buffy on the flanks and its black head shows a distinctive white stripe running from the bill over and behind the eye. In addition, these two species are almost identical in behavior, even in voice. The mountain chickadee call is harsher and a more variable *"cheeks-a-dee-zee-dee."* Both species are vigorous feeders, moving from twig to branch and branch to shrub in their search for insects. During the breeding season the mountain chickadee inhabits the coniferous forests to near timberline, leaving the valleys more or less to the black-capped. During the winter they often associate with black-capped and boreal chickadees in the valley bottoms. The mountain chickadee is a permanent resident throughout the Rockies except for the extreme north.

T. ULRICH

Common Raven

T. ULRICH

Black-capped Chickadee

T. ULRICH

Mountain Chickadee

✓Boreal Chickadee (11 cm)
Parus hudsonicus

The boreal chickadee is a lovely little bird with a brown cap, grayish brown above, and dusky white or light gray below with bright rufous sides. Its cheek patches are often dusky white and the throat patch is black. Long before you see it, you may hear its rather wheezy *"sick-a-day-day"* call notes. These birds prefer dense coniferous and mixedwood forests. The boreal chickadee nests in holes in stumps and dead trees, and lays its eggs on a bed of mammal fur, moss, and shreds of bark. Although fairly common residents throughout much of the Canadian Rockies, they move from low to higher altitudes in the spring with a reversal of direction in the autumn.

Red-breasted Nuthatch (10 cm)
Sitta canadensis

The red-breasted nuthatch has a pronounced white eyebrow stripe set off by a black line through the eye and black on the crown and neck. Its back, wings, and tail are mostly grayish blue. The rusty-colored underparts give this species its name. Females and juveniles have duller heads and paler underparts. The red-breasted nuthatch is often called "upside-down bird" because it may be seen crawling down a tree trunk in jerky, circular spirals. A greatly enlarged hind toe assists in this downward movement. This adaptation allows it to search nooks and crannies for bark-dwelling insects, eggs, and larvae overlooked by other birds which feed while moving in an upright fashion. They also feed on conifer seeds and readily capture flying insects for food when available. This nuthatch inhabits coniferous woods, preferring Douglas fir and pine forests. These birds smear pitch from conifers around the entrance of their nesting cavity. The function of this peculiar habit is unknown. They are fairly common year-long residents in the Rockies.

Brown Creeper (11 cm)
Certhia americana

Unlike the red-breasted nuthatch that spirals down the trunks of trees, the brown creeper starts at the bottom of a tree and climbs upward. After investigating every crack and crevice for insects and insect eggs hidden in the bark of conifers, they fly down to the base of another tree and start upward again. The brown creeper is a small, inconspicuous bird with camouflage colors and a faint voice. Its crown and upperparts are brown with grayish white streaks. Underparts are whitish with a buff tinge on the flanks and undertail. The long, stiff tail of pointed feathers is used as a prop as this creeper uses its sharp-pointed, downcurved bill like tweezers to pluck insects from the bark. Generally solitary, the brown creeper prefers mature coniferous and mixed woodlands. Their crescent-shaped nest is usually built under a piece of loose bark, but they occasionally use natural cavities and woodpecker holes. This creeper is a fairly common year-round resident in the central and southern parts of our area.

E. JONES

Boreal Chickadee

d-breasted Nuthatch

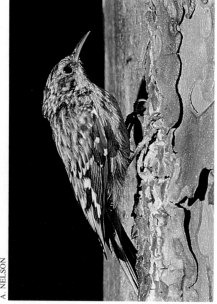

A. NELSON

Brown Creeper

Rock Wren (12 cm)
Salpinctes obsoletus

BJKCKW
WREN FAMILY

The rock wren is an energetic little bird that gives its presence away with a variety of loud notes and trills that carry a long distance. Their upperparts are grayish brown, finely speckled with white and black, with a small cinnamon patch on the lower back. The underparts are dull white becoming tinged with cinnamon on the flanks, lower belly, and undertail coverts. The breast is finely streaked. Their middle tail feathers are the same color as the back while the outer tail feathers are barred with black and buff toward the tips. These birds live in open, rocky areas where they probe the crevices and crannies for insects. They frequently bob their heads, especially when alarmed. These drab-colored birds nest in crannies of rocks and cliffs or on talus slopes. Although there are no nesting records, the rock wren is occasionally seen at low elevation during the spring and summer from Jasper south and probably does breed there.

House Wren (11 cm)
Troglodytes aedon

BJKCW
WREN FAMILY

The house wren is a busybody with irrepressible energy. It bustles hither and thither all day long scolding everyone and searching shrubbery and gardens for insects. It is also an indefatigable and exuberant singer over long periods of the day. The house wren lacks prominent field marks. It is grayish brown above and finely barred on the wings and tail. The throat and breast are a dull grayish white with a tinge of buff-gray and some faint barring on the sides and flanks. This wren likes deciduous thickets and shrubbery in open forests and a variety of man-made habitations. It utilizes a wide variety of cavities for nesting including bird boxes. They usually make a number of dummy nests in the vicinity of the real one. This aggressive little wren often steals into the nests of other birds in the neighborhood and punctures their eggs. The house wren is scarce throughout all but the northern portion of the Canadian Rockies.

Winter Wren (8 cm)
Troglodytes troglodytes

BJKCKWY
WREN FAMILY

The winter wren is much like the house wren except it is smaller, darker, has a shorter tail, and heavier barrings on the flanks. It has reddish brown upperparts and a stubby tail that is generally cocked-up over its back. There is a faint buff stripe present over the eye. This wren is one of the finest songsters in the Canadian Rockies with a typical song lasting from eight to ten seconds. It would easily go unnoticed as its pokes about on the forest floor except for its sustained song. The winter wren inhabits the densest and deepest coniferous forests. It also has a characteristic bobbing behavior as it feeds and flits among the brush piles. Males build nests in dense brush, under logs, in upturned tree roots, or in crevices of a bank, but generally near water. The often polygamous male may attract several females to different nests. Being a good parent, the male helps in feeding all the clutches produced. The winter wren is fairly common in the Rockies during the spring and summer.

T. ULRICH

ock Wren

House Wren

E. JONES

Winter Wren

American Dipper (14 cm)

Cinclus mexicanus

DIPPER FAMILY

The American dipper, or water ouzel as it is sometimes called, is the only aquatic songbird in North America. Dippers are plump, stubby-tailed, and sooty gray overall with a tinge of brown on the head and neck. They inhabit clear, cascading mountain streams up to timberline. The dipper is uniquely adapted to this watery habitat. A filmy outer plumage with a thick undercoat of down helps keep it warm. A very large preen gland provides oil to keep its feathers waterproof. This bird also has a movable flap over the nostrils to keep out water and transparent extra eyelids to protect the eyes from sprays of water. The short, stubby wings are used both in flight and to propel under water. When under water, the dipper walks along the stream bottom feeding on caddisflies, stoneflies, mayflies, mosquitoes, dragonflies, water beetles, and other water-dwelling insects and their larvae. While standing, most often on a spray-drenched rock, this bird rapidly raises and lowers its body by bending the legs, hence the name dipper. The dipper is a solitary bird except at nesting time and during the winter when it moves to the low valleys in search of open water. The nest of the dipper is a bulky, domed affair constructed of grasses and mosses and lined with leaves and rootlets. There is an entrance hole on the side. The nest is usually built near water on a rock, on a ledge behind a waterfall, or under a bridge. The melodious song of the dipper is bubbling and wrenlike and can be heard during all seasons of the year and in all kinds of weather. The song carries well even over rushing water. When disturbed, the dipper flies low over the water, winding with the stream. This bird is a common year-round resident within suitable habitat.

American Dipper

American Dipper

American Dipper (nestlings)

109

Golden-crowned Kinglet (9 cm)   BJKCKLWY
Regulus satrapa   OLD-WORLD WARBLER SUBFAMILY

A diminutive bird, the golden-crowned kinglet male has an orange crown
bordered first by lemon yellow, then black. The female has the orange totally
replaced by lemon yellow. Both sexes have a white line extending from over the
beak to above the eye and a black line through the eye. The rest of the upperparts
of this bird are grayish olive and marked with two white wing bars. The whitish
underparts are tinged with gray on the sides and flanks. Both the golden-crowned
and ruby-crowned kinglets have a habit of flicking their wings during momentary
pauses which is useful in separating them from warblers. The call of the golden-
crowned is a very high-pitched *"tsee-tsee-tsee"* and occasionally a single but
more prolonged *"tseee."* This kinglet is a common breeding bird throughout
coniferous forests in the Canadian Rockies. It is present in smaller numbers
during much of the winter.

Ruby-crowned Kinglet (10 cm)   BJKCKLWY
Regulus calendula   OLD-WORLD WARBLER SUBFAMILY

The ruby-crowned kinglet's dusky underparts, broken, whitish eye-ring, and lack
of stripes over the eye easily separate this species from the golden-crowned
kinglet. The male's ruby-colored crown patch is seldom visible. This kinglet's
song is clear and very loud for such a tiny creature. The characteristic song is a
"tee, chur, teedadee," each part repeated three times before proceeding with the
next. Often found in flocks in dense foliage, these kinglets are largely insect
eaters. They are common breeding birds throughout the Rockies, preferring
coniferous forests, mixed woodlands, and thickets of shrubs.

Golden-crowned Kinglet

Ruby-crowned Kinglet

Ruby-crowned Kinglet

✓Mountain Bluebird (15 cm)
Sialia currucoides

BJKCKLWY
THRUSH SUBFAMILY

Bluebirds are one of the harbingers of spring and a symbol of love, happiness, and renewed hope. The back, wing, and tail of the male mountain bluebird are a bright cerulean blue and the throat and breast are a paler blue which fades to white on the abdomen. On the female the wing and tail feathers are a bright sky blue and the head and back are uniformly gray-brown. Her throat is a brownish ash giving way to white on the lower breast and undertail coverts. Mountain bluebirds are primarily ground-feeders and consume a diet composed largely of insects. They have a habit of hovering, in a hawklike manner, a meter or more above the ground while searching the earth below for food. During spring migration, they can sometimes be seen strung along a barbed-wire fence like brilliant blue jewels. Cavities in trees, woodpecker excavations, crevices and cracks in hillsides, and birdhouses are used for nesting. The mountain bluebird is fairly common in open montane areas on the eastern slopes and scarce on the western slopes.

Townsend's Solitaire (17 cm)
Myadestes townsendi

BJKCKLWY
THRUSH SUBFAMILY

The Townsend's solitaire is a bird typical of high mountain areas, particularly open subalpine forests. This bird is a plain grayish brown above and decidedly paler below. It has a bold, dull white eye-ring. Both the burnt orange wing patches and the rather long tail, with largely white outertail feathers, are most conspicuous in flight. Its song is robinlike, but more sustained and delightful. Although the solitaire captures flying insects, it also feeds on berries and soft seeds. This solitaire nests on the ground, often under an overhang or some other kind of concealment. The Townsend's solitaire is a fairly common breeding bird in our area.

Mountain Bluebird (male)

Mountain Bluebird (female)

Townsend's Solitaire

113

Veery (15 cm)
Catharus fuscescens

The veery is the only thrush whose song *"da-vee-ur, vee-ur, veer, veer"* begins on a high note and ends on a low one. Its twilight song is flutelike, haunting, and beautifully peaceful. The bird itself is a reddish brown above and mostly white below. Its breast is suffused with buff and is lightly spotted with brown. Nests of this bird are on or near the ground. Much of the veery's time is spent on the ground searching under leaves for insects and on bushes for berries. The veery is an occasional bird of deciduous forests, especially those with dense undergrowth. It is not likely to be encountered north of Banff.

Swainson's Thrush (16 cm)
Catharus ustulatus

The Swainson's thrush is a uniformly gray-brown bird above with a heavily spotted, creamy buff breast, and both a buffy face and eye-ring. Thrushes are among the most gifted of all songsters. To hear the musically pleasing call of the Swainson's one must intrude into its territory during the freshness of early morning or the stillness of early evening because it generally sings only for a few minutes at dawn and dusk. Each phrase of the song is higher than the preceding one. Some birders characterize its song as *"oh, Aurelia, will ya, WILL YA."* This thrush feeds on the ground and in trees, eating insects and berries. Nesting within 2 m of the ground, the Swainson's thrush is a common summer resident in coniferous forests throughout our area.

Hermit Thrush (15 cm)
Catharus guttatus

Many bird lovers consider the hermit thrush to be the finest singer of all North American birds. Certainly the richness of tone and perfection of execution are equaled by few others. The hermit thrush has an olive brown back and a reddish brown rump and tail. Its face is a gray-brown with a thin, white eye-ring. The underparts are buff to whitish with large dark spots on the breast and streaks on the sides of the throat and flanks. Among the thrushes, the hermit has a distinct behavior characteristic. When landing or if disturbed it slowly raises the tail and flicks the wings. They generally nest and feed on the ground. This thrush favors coniferous forests or mixed woodlands. Hermit thrushes are common throughout the Rockies.

T. ULRICH

eery

Swainson's Thrush

E. JONES

Hermit Thrush

American Robin (22 cm)
Turdus migratorius

THRUSH SUBFAMILY

One of the best-known birds in North America, the American robin is a sign of spring to most communities within the Rockies. As the snowbanks melt, their familiar *"cheer-up"* or *"cheerily"* song is a prophecy of green grass and beautiful wildflowers soon to come. They have a number of other calls including a mating song accompanied by the male displaying and lifting his tail higher than his head and a scolding chirp accompanied by tail jerking. Almost too well-known to require much description, the male robin has a distinctive red-orange breast, a black head, white eye-ring, yellow bill with a black tip, black-and-white streaked throat, and a gray back. Females are paler in color. The female makes the cup-shaped nest of mud mixed with grasses, string, and small twigs. She works mud into place with her feet and bill, molding it with her body. Three or four turquoise blue eggs are laid in the grass-lined nest, typically in a tree crotch. As might be expected of such a ubiquitous species, the robin adapts to a wide variety of habitats from the bottom valleys to timberline. Robins are common breeding birds throughout our area.

Varied Thrush (20 cm)
Ixoreus naevius

BJKCKLWY
THRUSH SUBFAMILY

Much more secretive than the friendly American robin, the varied thrush prefers dense coniferous forests as habitat. Good field marks for the varied thrush are the orange eyebrow above a black mask, a dark slate gray head, and a black band across the tawny orange breast. The remainder of the upperparts are dark slate gray except for two, bold orange wing bars and orange wing stripes. Females are similar but duller in color. Its song is an eerie whistle in various pitches. Varied thrushes feed in the trees and among dead leaves on the ground, eating earthworms, insects, and a variety of ripe berries. They generally nest in dense coniferous forests. This thrush is common throughout the Canadian Rockies.

Water Pipit (14 cm)
Anthus spinoletta

BJKCKLWY
PIPIT FAMILY

In spring, a water pipit has a pale grayish back with faint dark streaks that are also on the crown. It has two buff wing bars and white outertail feathers like the dark-eyed junco. The underparts are rich buff with fine blackish streaks on the breast and flanks. The center of the belly and undertail coverts are slightly paler. Eyebrows are the same rich buff as the breast. Both the slender bill and legs are dark in color. If they can be seen, the long hind claws are distinctive. When feeding on the ground, they walk rather than hop and often dip their tails. Their *"pip-it"* and *"tsip-tsip"* calls will help in identifying this bird. On the alpine breeding grounds, the water pipit has the skylarklike habit of flying and singing high into the air and then descending in a perpendicular dive, like a falling stone. They nest on the ground above timberline, often under low vegetation or near a rock. The water pipit is a common breeding bird in alpine areas throughout the Rockies. They also use shores and fields with almost no vegetation during their spring and fall migrations.

116

American Robin

Varied Thrush

Water Pipit

117

Bohemian Waxwing (16 cm)

Bombycilla garrulus

BJKCKLWY

WAXWING FAMILY

Bohemian waxwings are a popular bird because of their elegant plumage, highly social nature, and occasional abundance near our homes. Adults are a soft brownish gray, generally brownest on the head and grayish on the abdomen and rump. They have a black mask around the eye, a black throat, a long, pointed crest on the head, and a yellow-tipped tail. An excellent field mark is the distinct, dark rusty undertail coverts. Bohemians have white and yellow wing markings. At very close range you may see brilliant red appendages, like sealing wax, on the enlarged tips of the secondaries. These birds congregate in large numbers in the fall and descend upon towns to strip fruit from trees and shrubs. They chatter constantly, giving a high-pitched *"zlrrr"* call, as they feast and then swirl to the top of a nearby tree. They nest in open coniferous and mixed woodlands, generally in a coniferous tree. This bird is a year-round resident and is most common during the fall and winter months.

Cedar Waxwing (15 cm)

Bombycilla cedrorum

BJKCKLWY

WAXWING FAMILY

The cedar waxwing is very similar to the Bohemian waxwing. Cedar waxwings have white undertail coverts rather than dark rusty ones, the abdomen, flanks, and sides are pale yellow instead of soft gray, and they lack the white and yellow markings on the wings. They use a great variety of habitats; the most important requirement seems to be having berry bushes and small-fruit trees in the vicinity. They also devour a variety of insects. Cedar waxwings nest in the branches of coniferous and deciduous trees and in tall shrubs. Waiting for the wild berry crop to ripen, these birds are among the last of the spring migrants to start nesting. Their voice is similar to the Bohemian waxwing but is higher pitched. Cedar waxwings are seen in the Rockies only in the summer rather than year-round as with the Bohemians. Cedar waxwings are fairly common in the southern portion of our area; they are scarce in the north.

Northern Shrike (20 cm)

Lanius excubitor

BJKCKLWY

SHRIKE FAMILY

The northern shrike is an interesting example of a songbird adapted for a predatory life. Its bill is hooked with a notch and tooth at the tip of the upper mandible. However, this shrike lacks the powerful feet of other raptors to hold its prey while tearing it apart. The victim is often impaled on a thorn or barbed wire or jammed between branches to be torn apart and eaten. Small mammals and birds are taken as food; insects are an important part of the summer diet. Northern shrikes are somewhat two-toned, slightly barred white below, and light bluish gray above with sharply contrasting black-and-white wings and tail. They are best identified by a narrow, black face mask around the eye with a whitish line above. These birds nest in the extreme northern portion of the Rockies and overwinter in the southern portion. Whether a migrant, breeding bird, or winter resident, the northern shrike is scarce.

Bohemian Waxwing

Northern Shrike

E. JONES

T. ULRICH

Cedar Waxwing

European Starling (15 cm)

Sturnus vulgaris

STARLING FAMILY

Introduced into North America in 1890, the European starling has flourished and spread across much of the continent. This adaptable species now breeds throughout most of the Rockies. The aggressive nature of the starling has taken a toll on native birds by competing with them for choice nesting holes. European starlings change plumage with the seasons. In the spring its entire body is black with metallic purple and green iridescence, and it has a yellow bill and dull reddish legs. After the breeding season its bill is dark and the starling is heavily speckled with white and buff marks, except on the wings and tail. At all seasons they have short, squared tails, pointed triangular wings, and stocky bodies. Immature birds are a uniform mouse brown. Starlings are great mimics and give a wide medley of chirps, squeaks, warbles, and twitterings resembling the calls and songs of other birds. Their diet includes a variety of insects, seeds, and fruits. Usually found in flocks, the starling is present year-round from Jasper south and is a summer resident to the north in the Rockies. They are most common near towns within our area.

Solitary Vireo (12 cm)

Vireo solitarius

BJKCKLWY

VIREO FAMILY

The solitary vireo is a conspicuously marked bird. Distinct white lores and eye-rings give this bird a spectacled look. It has two decidedly whitish wing bars, also. The Rocky Mountain race of solitary vireos are dark gray above, with at most a very light suffusion of yellow on the flanks. Solitary vireos generally feed at treetop level, eating a variety of caterpillars, moths, and insects. The male helps to build the hanging nest and with incubation of the eggs. This sweet-singing vireo has a rich and variable song ranging from two to six phrases and a wrenlike, scolding call. They prefer open forests with a mixture of coniferous and deciduous trees. As implied by its name, the solitary vireo is rarely seen in flocks. It breeds throughout most of the Rockies.

Warbling Vireo (12 cm)

Vireo gilvus

BJKCKLWY

VIREO FAMILY

Warbling vireos are smoky gray on the upperwing parts with a tinge of olive green on the back and rump. They have a faint white eyebrow and a faint dusky eyeline. Underparts are white with a tinge of pale yellowish buff on the sides and flanks. This nondescript vireo, hidden in the leafy treetops, is often detected and identified only by its song. Its song is a continuous musical warble, often gradually rising in pitch and intensity. Some birders characterize the song as *"bring it here, bring it here, BRING IT."* Showing a decided preference for deciduous trees, the warbling vireo feeds almost exclusively on insects. Its well-made, cup-shaped nest is usually suspended from the fork of two branches in a deciduous tree. This vireo is a common breeding bird throughout most of the Rockies.

European Starling

Solitary Vireo

Warbling Vireo

Red-eyed Vireo (13 cm)

BJKCKLWY

Vireo olivaceus

VIREO FAMILY

Adult red-eyed vireos have a slate gray crown with the remaining upperparts a dark olive green. The well-defined white stripe over the eye is bordered above with black and with a conspicuous dusky streak below. These markings on the face make the best field marks. The red iris, as implied by the name, can be seen only at close range. The white underparts are masked with yellowish olive on the sides and flanks. The red-eyed vireo is a frequenter of aspen and poplar groves, where it would usually go unnoticed except for the continuous song. Few birds are more vocal than this vireo. The endless and repetitive vocalization has given the species the name of "preacher-bird." The red-eyed vireo generally nests in a deciduous tree or shrub not more than 3 m above the ground. They are fairly common breeding birds throughout the Rockies, sometimes in small, loose colonies.

Tennessee Warbler (11 cm)

BJKCKLWY

Vermivora peregrina

WOOD-WARBLER SUBFAMILY

The Tennessee warbler is a plain and undistinguished bird. Breeding males have forest green upperparts except for the blue-gray crown and nape. They have a bold white eyebrow with a dusky line through the eye. Their underparts are white. Females have a greener crown and the eyebrow, throat, and upper breast are masked with yellow. Breeding males have slimmer bills and greener backs than the red-eyed and warbling vireos with which they may be confused. In addition, they are much more active and restless. Regularly feeding far up in the foliage, the Tennessee warbler could go unnoticed if the male did not sing. Although he may not sing well, his song is one of the loudest of the warblers. The song is high-pitched and typically three-parted. Their favorite nesting haunts are clumps of aspen and spruce near marshes, larch swamps, and muskeg borders. This warbler nests on the ground. Tennessee warblers are fairly common breeding birds from Kananaskis northward.

Orange-crowned Warbler (11 cm)

BJKCKLWY

Vermivora celata

WOOD-WARBLER SUBFAMILY

The orange-crowned warbler is a tiny, drab bird that attracts little attention. It has unmarked, olive green upperparts with paler undersides that have faint dusky streakings on the breast. Its undertail coverts are yellow. Also present are greenish yellow eyebrows and a partial yellow eye-ring. The tawny orange crown is seldom discernible in the field. The species name *celata,* meaning concealed or hidden, refers to those hidden head feathers. Orange-crowned are distinguished from Tennessee warblers by the yellow undertail coverts, streaks on the breast, thinner slightly downcurved bill, and larger tail. The song of the orange-crowned warbler is a weak trill that does not carry far. They frequent thickets of shrubs near rivers and wetlands, typically nesting on the ground but occasionally in low bushes. This warbler is a common breeding bird throughout our area.

E. JONES

Red-eyed Vireo

E. JONES

Tennessee Warbler

E. JONES

Orange-crowned Warbler

Yellow Warbler (10 cm)

Dendroica petechia

BJKCKLWY
WOOD-WARBLER SUBFAMILY

The yellow warbler was well named for it is essentially all yellow both above and below, the yellowest of its family. Males have bold rusty streaks on their sides and breasts; females generally show just a faint trace of such marks. The dark eye is prominent in the uniformly yellow face. Both sexes have yellow tails with spots. They sing exuberantly with highly variable songs. Some interpretations include *"sweet-sweet-sweetsweet-sweet-sweeter-sweeter"* and *"tseet-tseet-tseetsitta-sitta-see."* The yellow warbler breeds in thickets of willows and alders near streamsides, lakes, and other shrubby areas. Their nest is a deep, felted cup placed in the crotch of a bush or small tree. Such nests are frequently parasitized by brown-headed cowbirds who do not build nests, but lay their eggs in the nests of other birds. Sometimes refusing to incubate the intruding egg or eggs, the yellow warbler builds a new floor over the old one burying the entire contents, including its own eggs, under the new structure. Yellow warblers are common breeding birds throughout the Rockies.

Magnolia Warbler (11 cm)

Dendroica magnolia

BJKCKLY
WOOD-WARBLER SUBFAMILY

This handsome black-and-yellow warbler is a rare migrant through the southern and central Rockies. Its breeding range includes the northern Rockies. Black spruce muskegs, young and open conifer stands, and mixedwoods are its preferred breeding habitats. Breeding males have bluish gray heads and napes, black backs, and yellow rumps. The sides of their heads are black with conspicuous white eyebrows. The underparts are yellow, except for white undertail coverts and they have a black-streaked necklace across the breast, with the streakings extending far down the sides. The wings have two prominent white bars. Distinct from all other warblers in the Canadian Rockies is the broad white tail band, which shows in flight. Females are similar but duller in color. Its song is weak and variable.

Yellow-rumped Warbler (12 cm)

Dendroica coronata

BJKCKLWY
WOOD-WARBLER SUBFAMILY

The yellow-rumped warbler consists of two races, the Audubon's and Myrtle, which were formerly considered separate species. Audubon's has a yellow throat and the Myrtle a white throat. They both have the basic identifying marks of yellow on the crown, rump, and sides. The new species name *coronata* refers to the yellow crown that both races have in common. The males are blue-gray above, have white on the outer tail, large white wing patches, and black breast marks. Females have the same basic patterns but are more brownish above with two wing bars. Yellow-rumped warblers are largely insectivorous but they feed on fruits and seeds when insects are scarce. The yellow-rumped is probably the most abundant warbler in the Canadian Rockies. During the nesting season they prefer open coniferous forests with a few deciduous trees, particularly near water. Although they breed throughout our area, interbreeding of the two races is particularly common in the Banff and Jasper regions.

Yellow Warbler

Magnolia Warbler

Yellow-rumped Warbler

Townsend's Warbler (11 cm)
Dendroica townsendi

BJKCKLWY
WOOD-WARBLER SUBFAMILY

Preferring dense standings of fir and spruce as breeding and feeding habitat, the Townsend's warbler could easily go undetected among the tops of tall trees if it were not for the male's wheezy song. It is generally composed of five to ten *"sweet"* or *"zee"* notes with a gradual rise in pitch toward the end. It would be a pity to miss this highly contrastive yellow-and-black warbler. Adult males have black crowns, cheeks, throats, and upper breasts. Broad, bright yellow stripes over the eye and on the side of the throat border the black cheek patch. There is a small yellow spot under the eye as well. The remainder of the upperparts are olive green spotted and streaked with black. There are two white bars on the wings and the outer tail feathers are marked with white. This warbler has a yellow lower breast, white belly, and the flanks and sides are streaked with black. Adult females are similar but with more green on the back, head, and sides and a much larger yellow throat area. Townsend's warblers breed throughout the Rockies.

Blackpoll Warbler (12 cm)
Dendroica striata

BJKCKLY
WOOD-WARBLER SUBFAMILY

A solid black crown, black mustache, and white cheeks and underparts will identify a breeding male blackpoll warbler in the spring. Both the back and sides are boldly streaked with black, and there are two white wing bars. Breeding females are more olive colored above with dusky streaking, lack the mustache, have paler stripes on the sides, and often have a yellowish tinge to the wing bars. The species name *striata* means striped and refers to the many stripes on the back, sides, and flanks of these birds. Both sexes have white spots near the tips of the outer tail feathers. Fall birds are very similar to breeding females but lack the head streaks and have a yellowish tinge below. Extremely high pitched and monotonous, the male blackpoll's *"tsit-tsit-TSIT-tsit-tsit"* song grows in volume toward the middle and then softens toward the end. They are common breeders in young conifer stands from Banff north. They are spring and fall migrants to the south of Banff.

American Redstart (11 cm)
Setophaga ruticilla

BJKCKLWY
WOOD-WARBLER SUBFAMILY

The American redstart is one of the handsomest and most active of the warblers in the Rockies. Mature males are glossy black with blaze orange patches on the wings, sides, and tail. Their bellies and undertail coverts are white. Full adult male plumage, as described, is not acquired until after their first breeding season. Females have gray heads, olive gray backs, dull white underparts, yellowish orange on the flanks and sides, and yellow patches on the wings and basal half of the tail. Year-old males have salmon-colored breasts with some black spotting. A male redstart is in constant motion flitting from twig to twig, fanning his tail, spreading his wings, and displaying his brilliant orange patches against his ebony plumage. Redstarts are strictly insectivorous. For nesting, American redstarts like deciduous woodlands with shrubbery, particularly stream banks lined with dense alder and willow thickets. They breed throughout our area.

E. JONES

Townsend's Warbler

Blackpoll Warbler

T. ULRICH

American Redstart

Northern Waterthrush (13 cm)   BJKCKLWY
Seiurus noveboracensis   WOOD-WARBLER SUBFAMILY

As implied by its name, the northern waterthrush in some ways looks and acts like a thrush and is often found near water. Its small size, line over the eye, teetering motions, streaked instead of spotted underparts, and warblerlike bill distinguish it from real thrushes. This waterthrush has unmarked, dark olive brown upperparts and whitish underparts tinged with yellow on the breast and abdomen. The throat is spotted and the breast and sides are heavily streaked with dark brown. A prominent white line extends over the eye and ear. Except for singing males, waterthrushes stay mostly on the ground, preferring woodland bogs, swamps, and dense thickets. They walk rather than hop and have a teetering motion similar to that described for the spotted sandpiper. During the nesting season the male selects a perch in the treetops and sings a high-pitched *"hurry-hurry-hurry-pretty-pretty-pretty"* song. The northern waterthrush is occasional in wooded swamps. It breeds throughout the Rockies, often nesting in the upturned roots of a fallen tree or on the ground in a stream bank hollow.

MacGillivray's Warbler (12 cm)   BJKCKLWY
Oporornis tolmiei   WOOD-WARBLER SUBFAMILY

In breeding plumage the adult male has a slate gray head, neck, and throat, turning to black on the breast with bold white crescents both above and below the eye. The remaining upperparts are olive green, while the rest of the underparts are bright lemon yellow. Breeding females are similar but much duller except for a whitish gray throat and a yellow breast. Shy and secretive, the MacGillivray's warbler lives and feeds in dense thickets of shrubs. Any area with low, dense undergrowth such as avalanche slopes, logged-over areas, burns, and stream banks are favored habitats. The female builds her nest in dense shrubs, generally near the ground. The MacGillivray's song has two parts and may be interpreted as *"sweet-sweet-sweet, peachy-peachy."* It breeds throughout our area.

Common Yellowthroat (11 cm)   BJKCKLWY
Geothlypis trichas   WOOD-WARBLER SUBFAMILY

The male common yellowthroat, with his broad jet black mask extending from the bill over the eyes and across the cheeks to the side of the neck, is an easy bird to recognize. The black mask is bordered by a whitish gray line above and a bright yellow chin, throat, and breast below. The belly is whitish and the undertail coverts are yellow. The upperparts are olive brown. Lacking the black mask, the female has a dark olive brown face, crown, back, and wings with pale whitish yellow eye-rings. Her breast is usually yellow with browner flanks and a whitish belly. The male's song is generally a *"witchity-witchity-witchity"* but with innumerable variations depending on the individual bird and where it is found. It also gives a repeated, wrenlike *"tscick"* of disapproval to intruders within its domain. Almost any damp, brushy place will attract common yellowthroats. They generally nest on or very near the ground, usually near water. The yellowthroat is a common breeding bird throughout the Rockies.

E. JONES

Northern Waterthrush

E. JONES

MacGillivray's Warbler

E. JONES

Common Yellowthroat

Wilson's Warbler (11 cm)

BJKCKLWY

Wilsonia pusilla

WOOD-WARBLER SUBFAMILY

This pretty, little yellow warbler is usually a bird of the shrubbery rather than of the trees. Adult male Wilson's warblers have a small black cap and a yellowish face. The remaining upperparts are plain olive green except for the tail which is dark above and below. All the underparts are yellow. In females and immatures the black crown is lacking or partly obscured by greenish feather edgings. Both sexes have conspicuous dark eyes in an otherwise unmarked face. Their song has been interpreted as a *"CHI-CHI-CHI-CHI-chet-chet,"* dropping downward in pitch toward the end. When the Wilson's warbler is perched, it has a habit of twitching its tail. The favored breeding habitats of this warbler are alder swales, flooded willow bottomlands, avalanche slopes, and other shrubby areas along streams, ponds, and marshes. Most of these warblers nest on the ground, often at the base of a bush or sapling. They are fairly common breeding birds throughout the Rockies.

Western Tanager (16 cm)

BJKCKLWY

Piranga ludoviciana

TANAGER FAMILY

The striking, brilliant western tanager is one of the most beautiful birds within the Canadian Rockies. Showy males are bright yellow with black wings, upper back, and tail and a red head and face. Females, larger than the males, are a dull greenish color above and yellow below. Both sexes have two yellow or white wing bars and a short, stout, thick, yellowish bill. Western tanagers are birds of the upper forest canopy. They are quiet feeders, often waiting for insects to come to them, and not very active birds. The western tanager is, therefore, often located by the robinlike song that it sings from an exposed perch in the high canopy. Western tanagers are fairly common breeding birds in open coniferous, mixed, and deciduous forests throughout our area. They usually nest among the higher branches in conifers.

Lazuli Bunting (11 cm)

BJKCKWY

Passerina amoena

CARDINAL FAMILY

The strongly contrasting, brilliant coloration of the male lazuli bunting is unmistakable. He has a cerulean blue head, neck, throat, and rump; darker blue back and wings; two bold white bars on the wings; rich cinnamon across the breast and part-way down the flanks; and a white belly. The much more sedate female is grayish brown above with a grayish blue rump and buff on the throat and breast fading to white on the abdomen and undertail coverts. She has two buff to whitish wing bars. Both sexes have stubby, heavy bills that are very different from the slender bills of bluebirds. Dense thickets of rosebush, chokecherry, saskatoon, alder, willow, or aspen groves with abundant undergrowth seem to be equally attractive habitats for the lazuli bunting. This bunting is fairly common in the extreme southern portion of the Canadian Rockies and is only occasional north of Banff.

Wilson's Warbler

Western Tanager

Lazuli Bunting

131

Chipping Sparrow (12 cm)

Spizella passerina

BJKCKLWY

NEW-WORLD SPARROW SUBFAMILY

The breeding plumage of the dapper, little male chipping sparrow includes a bright rufous cap set off by a conspicuous white eyebrow, strong black eyeline through the lores to the dark bill, and unmarked grayish white underparts. Its back and wings are light brown streaked with black. The wings have two whitish wing bars and the tail is sharply notched. Females are often duller and the rufous crown is frequently streaked with black. The *"chip"* call, from which this bird's name is derived, is a series of rapid, unaccented notes that are often delivered from the outermost tip of a conifer branch or small shrub. Chipping sparrows are common in openings of coniferous and mixedwood forests and in the vicinity of human dwellings. They feed on or close to the ground. This tame little sparrow breeds throughout the Canadian Rockies, building its hair-lined nest on the branch of a conifer.

Clay-colored Sparrow (11 cm)

Spizella pallida

BJKCKWY

NEW-WORLD SPARROW SUBFAMILY

The head of the clay-colored sparrow has a strongly contrasting pattern. Its brown crown is sharply streaked with black and has a distinct whitish central stripe. In addition, it has broad whitish eyebrows and malar stripes. The brown cheek patches are bordered by darker brown. Their buffy brown back and wings are sharply streaked with black. Two faint whitish bars are present on the wings and the forked tail is brown with gray edges. The unmarked underparts are white, masked with buff on the flanks and sides. Clay-colored sparrows have a distinctive song that is flat and an insectlike *"bzzzz"* repeated two to ten times. That song is generally delivered from a low perch in an opening. This sparrow is a bird of open spaces near wetlands in the montane zone. It breeds throughout much of our area.

Brewer's Sparrow (11 cm)

Spizella breweri

BJKCKWY

NEW-WORLD SPARROW SUBFAMILY

In appearance the Brewer's is nearly identical to the clay-colored sparrow except that it lacks the white line down the crest of the crown and gray on the hind neck. The sides of the head of the Brewer's sparrow are more softly blended and it has a faint whitish eye-ring. In song and habitat preference these sparrows are very different. Songs of the Brewer's are varied, elaborate, and canarylike with a series of long, sweet musical trills added to the insectlike *"bzzz."* The Brewer's sparrow breeds in the subalpine or alpine zones, often nesting in stunted conifers or shrubs near timberline. In the Canadian Rockies, they generally breed from Jasper southward.

Chipping Sparrow

Clay-colored Sparrow

Brewer's Sparrow

Vesper Sparrow (14 cm)

BJKCKLWY

Pooecetes gramineus

NEW-WORLD SPARROW SUBFAMILY

This grayish sparrow is most readily identifiable by the display of white outer feathers on its dark brown tail, a feature that can be obscured except in flight. A chestnut shoulder patch is prominent on most individuals but is not present on all birds. It has a noticeably white eye-ring and brown cheek patch on the face, two pale wing bars, dull white underparts streaked with brown, and the legs are a flesh pink. Vesper sparrows have a very sweet song consisting of two low notes, then two higher ones followed by descending but rapid trills, always sung from an elevated perch. Some birders describe the song as *"here-here-WHERE-WHERE-all together down the hill."* This sparrow is a bird of open country and in the mountains it is restricted to dry grasslands at low elevations. They build a cup-shaped nest in a small hollow on the ground. The vesper sparrow is an occasional breeding bird throughout all but the extreme northern portion of the Rockies.

Savannah Sparrow (12 cm)

BJKCKLWY

Passerculus sandwichensis

NEW-WORLD SPARROW SUBFAMILY

Shy and lacking strong distinguishing marks, the savannah sparrow is easy for the casual observer to miss. This heavily streaked brown sparrow has a yellow lore with the yellow color often extending back to the pale eyebrow, a narrow yellow-white crown stripe, a dark whisker stripe, and is yellowish at the bend of the wing. There is generally a spot in the middle of the streaked breast. It has a short, slightly forked tail and pinkish legs and feet. There are several recognized races so the plumage can be highly variable. Like the vesper sparrow, the savannah is primarily a ground bird but it prefers moist sites up to timberline with a dense cover of grasses. The savannah usually stays on or near the ground and the best evidence of its presence is the weak, lispy song best described as *"tsip tsip tsip tsip wheeeeeeeee-you."* When flushed, this bird flies low and swift for a short distance before dropping suddenly back into the grass. They often run mouselike through the matted grasses before flushing. Their nest is a scratched-out hollow on the ground lined with grasses. The savannah sparrow is a common breeding bird throughout the Rockies.

Le Conte's Sparrow (11 cm)

JKCKW

Ammodramus leconteii

NEW-WORLD SPARROW SUBFAMILY

A secretive bird, the Le Conte's sparrow often scurries through dense grasses like a mouse. If this bird does take off, it flies briefly just above the vegetation before nipping back into dense cover. Learning the weak, hissing *"tse bzzzzz"* song is the best way to find this relatively colorful sparrow. The Le Conte's sparrow has a white central crown stripe on top of a blackish head, a pale orange face and breast, blue-gray ear patches, a bluish bill, and a short tail. Its breast and flanks are streaked with black. This sparrow is rare to scarce in marshes and other tall, rank grassland areas on the eastern slopes of the Rockies north to Jasper. Although there are breeding records from Jasper, most records are from the foothills, where it nests on or near the ground.

E. JONES

Vesper Sparrow

T. ULRICH

Savannah Sparrow

E. JONES

Le Conte's Sparrow

135

Fox Sparrow (16 cm)
Passerella iliaca

BJKCKLWY

NEW-WORLD SPARROW SUBFAMILY

The largest sparrow in the Canadian Rockies, the fox sparrow can be distinctly foxy red, as suggested by the common name of the species. However, different races of the fox sparrow occur in the Rockies with varied colorations. Adults of the reddish race have rusty red wings and tail, gray in varying degrees on the head and back, and a white throat and underparts. Adults of the grayish race have a gray head, back, and underparts with a rusty red tail. Both races have very heavy streaking on the throat and breast in the form of inverted Vs that point toward the throat. Those streaks sometimes aggregate to form a dark spot in the center of the breast. Fox sparrows are fairly common breeding birds throughout the Rockies in stunted conifers at timberline, shrubby avalanche slopes, and dense thickets in the subalpine zone.

Song Sparrow (14 cm)
Melospiza melodia

BJKCKLWY

NEW-WORLD SPARROW SUBFAMILY

Like the fox sparrow, there is considerable variation among the numerous races of song sparrows. Adults have brown upperparts with streaks of black, and two inconspicuous whitish wing bars. The brown head has a gray stripe behind the eye and along the lower edge of the cheek, and a heavy dark brown stripe bordering the sides of the throat. This sparrow's white underparts are streaked with dark brown or black. Those streaks aggregate on the breast in a center spot. In flight the bird vigorously pumps its rather long, round-ended tail up and down. Their sprightly song is delivered from boulders, shrubs, fences, trees, and even in flight. Females often sing before nesting. Largely ground feeders, the song sparrow's diet includes insects and the seeds of grasses and weeds. They are a common bird in shrubby wetlands and meadows, at the edge of clearings, near aspen groves, and in towns within the montane zone. This bird breeds throughout the Rockies, usually nesting on the ground.

Lincoln's Sparrow (12 cm)
Melospiza lincolnii

BJKCKLWY

NEW-WORLD SPARROW SUBFAMILY

The Lincoln's sparrow is a skulker and is extremely adept at keeping out of sight. It sings from cover and, generally, only alert birders who recognize the bubbling *"kee kee kee, see, see, see-dle see-dle see-dle, see-see-see-see"* song will detect its presence. Intruders on the breeding grounds, however, may be warned with rapid "chips" of alarm. The best field marks to distinguish the Lincoln's from other sparrows are the broad, buffy band across the breast and down the sides, which is streaked with black, and the narrow buffy white eye-rings. Its whitish belly is unmarked. The central gray head stripe is bordered by broad stripes of dark brown streaked with black. It also has a prominent, broad, gray eyebrow. The remaining upperparts are olive brown streaked with black and gray. Lincoln's sparrows have short, grayish brown tails with round ends. During the breeding season this sparrow prefers muskegs, moist wetlands, and stream banks with a cover of alders and willows. Nesting on the ground, this shy little sparrow is a common breeding bird throughout our area.

J. WASSINK

Fox Sparrow

T. ULRICH

Song Sparrow

E. JONES

Lincoln's Sparrow

White-throated Sparrow (15 cm)   BJKCLW
Zonotrichia albicollis   NEW-WORLD SPARROW SUBFAMILY

White-throated sparrows may have black and white or black and tan head stripes.
Its upperparts are chestnut brown streaked with black and two white wing bars.
The rump and long, notched tail are brown. Among the best identifying
characteristics are the well-defined white throat and the yellow spot between the
bill and eye. The breast and sides are gray and the olive flanks are lightly
streaked. Its bill is mostly dark. These sparrows have a rich, slow song that is
often paraphrased as *"I-love-Canada, Canada, Canada."* What a patriotic bird!
They spend much of their time on the ground scratching among the leaves for
insects and weed seeds. They also eat wild fruits. White-throated sparrows like
the margins of deciduous and mixedwood forests and brushy openings within the
montane zone. They are occasional breeders from Banff northward.

Golden-crowned Sparrow (17 cm)   BJKCKL
Zonotrichia atricapilla   NEW-WORLD SPARROW SUBFAMILY

The regal, golden-crowned sparrow is typical of alpine meadows near timberline.
As suggested by its common name, this sparrow has a golden crown patch
bordered on the forehead and sides of the face by broad, jet black stripes. It has a
brownish back streaked with darker brown; grayish brown breast, flanks and
sides; and a whitish belly. In addition, it has a long tail, inconspicuous white eye-
rings, and a bill that is dusky above and pale below. They are another ground-
feeding sparrow, eating various insects and seeds, and any threat will scatter them
into the nearest thicket. Their song is a slow three-noted *"oh, dear me."* Golden-
crowned sparrows nest near timberline in the alpine and subalpine zones. They
are a fairly common breeding bird northward from Banff National Park, nesting
on the ground or in dwarf shrubs.

White-crowned Sparrow (15 cm)   BJKCKLWY
Zonotrichia leucophrys   NEW-WORLD SPARROW SUBFAMILY

The bold black-and-white crown of the white-crowned sparrow distinguishes it
from all but the white-throated. Its pale bill, lack of a yellow spot between the
bill and eye, and the lack of a well-defined white throat patch distinguishes it
from the latter. White-crowned sparrows have a brown back, brown wings with
two white bars, and a gray face, neck, and breast. When excited, the head
feathers can be raised to form a low crest. Their song is a series of beautifully
whistled notes followed by buzzing trills. White-crowned are not nearly as shy as
golden-crowned sparrows and can often be studied at close range. Most of their
feeding is conducted on the ground. They are a common breeding bird from the
lower valleys to alpine meadows throughout the Canadian Rockies. Their major
habitat requirements are dense thickets of shrubs in open situations. They nest on
or near the ground under clumps of shrubs.

White-throated Sparrow

Golden-crowned Sparrow

White-crowned Sparrow

139

Dark-eyed Junco (13 cm)
Junco hyemalis

Dark-eyed juncos are active ground-dwellers that are sparrow-sized and shaped. Distinctive field marks include a pink bill; a black or gray hood and breast, sharply set off from the white belly; dark eyes; and white outer tail feathers that are obvious only when the bird flies. The dark-eyed junco includes several races and hybridization is common, producing a confusing range of colors. Dark gray heads, backs, breasts, flanks, and sides are characteristic of the slate-colored race found on the eastern slopes. The Oregon race with a black head, brown back, and pinkish flanks and sides may also be encountered. During the nesting season, the dark-eyed junco prefers openings and edges of coniferous and mixed woodland forests. They are common breeding birds throughout the Rockies, generally nesting on the ground from the bottom of the valleys to timberline. Some birds overwinter in the extreme southern portion of our area.

Lapland Longspur (15 cm)
Calcarius lapponicus

Lapland longspurs are observed in the spring as they pass through to the arctic tundra for nesting. The breeding plumage of the male is especially striking at that time. He has a black face and throat, a chestnut nape, a white stripe on the side of the head and neck, and white underparts. Females are more nondescript with a buff eyebrow, brown ear patch outlined in black, a rufous nape, and dark streaks on the throat, upper breast, and sides. Starting about late August, another influx of longspurs pass through heading south, but this time they are clothed in their dull fall plumage. Males at this time resemble summer-plumage females, having no black on their heads. Winter females lack the rufous napes, and the buff-colored chest and crown are streaked. A characteristic, long hind toenail, from which longspurs get their common name, is an excellent feature to identify this group of birds. These transients are occasionally seen in our area, mingling and feeding with horned larks and snow buntings.

Snow Bunting (15 cm)
Plectrophenax nivalis

The snow bunting is a sure sign of winter in the central parts of the Canadian Rockies, often arriving just prior to the first snow of autumn. At that time the adults are white with varying amounts of buff on the head and rump, the upperparts are a mottled beige and black, and the underparts are white. Snow buntings, or "snowbirds" as they are commonly called, spend all winter in parts of the foothills and front ranges. Before returning to the arctic tundra for nesting in the spring, their head and underparts are white, the bill and back are black, and the wings and tail are white and black. Mixed flocks of snow buntings, horned larks, and Lapland longspurs are often seen feeding together during migration. Snow buntings are a common winter resident in the central part of the Rockies; they are rare in the south and migrate through the northern portion.

Dark-eyed Junco

Lapland Longspur

Snow Bunting

Red-winged Blackbird (18 cm)
Agelaius phoeniceus

The red-winged blackbird is one of the most numerous birds on the North American continent. Everyone who notices birds knows this blackbird. The conspicuous and self-revealing male, who flies by to display his colors and to announce his presence with a cheerful *"konk-keREEE,"* could hardly be overlooked. The adult male is entirely glossy black except for bright red shoulder patches or epaulets with a yellow to buffy white border. Females are a sober brown above with paler underparts that are heavily streaked with blackish brown. Immatures are similar to adult females. Upon his arrival in the spring, the male establishes a territory and defends it aggressively against intruders. Freshwater marshes and water edges with a thick growth of cattails, bulrushes, sedges, and small trees are favored for nesting. Their concealed nests are loosely woven of marsh vegetation and lined with finer grasses. In late summer and fall vast flocks of these birds can do immense damage to grain crops, but during the summer they are largely insectivorous. Red-winged blackbirds are common in marshes throughout the Rockies.

Western Meadowlark (22 cm)
Sturnella neglecta

Although the American robin may be the harbinger of spring to city folks, the early-arriving western meadowlark serves that role for farmers and ranchers of the prairies. The meadowlark is not a true lark at all but related to the blackbirds and orioles. They have a very distinctive song as well as definitive markings. Delivered from a fencepost or rock, the cheery song generally has two distinct phrases that sound like *"Salt Lake City, is a very fine city,"* with many variants. The throat, breast, and abdomen are bright yellow with a contrasting, jet black V on the upper breast. Both the head and upperparts are mottled buffs, browns, and blacks and the wings and tail are barred with brown. When on the ground the western meadowlark flicks its tail incessantly; in flight, usually low over the ground, the white center-tail feathers are displayed. They are an occasional breeding bird of grasslands in the foothills and lower mountain valleys of the front range and near the Rocky Mountain Trench.

Yellow-headed Blackbird (22 cm)
Xanthocephalus xanthocephalus

The male yellow-headed blackbird is one of the most strikingly garbed birds of marshland environments. His yellowish orange head, neck, and chest and the broad white wing patches contrast sharply with the black body and tail. The female is a sooty brown above and yellow below. Their song is a harsh and unmusical variety of chirps, buzzes, and whistles which may be interpreted as *"kleep-kleep-a-ah-oo,"* or something similar. Yellow-headed blackbirds have very specific habitat preferences. They will only nest in emergent vegetation of cattails, bulrushes, and reeds, with shallow water below. They are occasional migrants through eastern slope wetlands in the spring and are rare on the western slopes to about the Peace River. There are only a few nesting records within the Rockies.

Red-winged Blackbird

Western Meadowlark

Yellow-headed Blackbird

Rusty Blackbird (22 cm)

BJKCKLY

Euphagus carolinus

BLACKBIRD/COWBIRD SUBFAMILY

In breeding plumage the male rusty blackbird is dull black with faint, glossy green iridescence. In the autumn the male has a rust crown, buff eyebrow, and rufous edgings on the feathers of the back, breast, and wings. Both sexes have pale, straw yellow eyes and sharply pointed bills. Breeding females are a plain, dull slate gray with darker upperparts. By autumn the females are masked with a rusty brown and the underparts are tipped with paler brown or buff. "Rusties" are very similar to Brewer's blackbirds. Breeding male rusties are much less glossy than Brewer's males, and female rusties have yellow rather than brown eyes. In autumn both sexes are much more heavily blotched with rusty browns than are Brewer's. Rusty blackbirds like wet woodlands with tall shrubs and standing water, such as beaver dams, stream edges, and muskeg bogs. They are spring and autumn transients to Jasper and occasional breeding birds farther north.

Brewer's Blackbird (20 cm)

BJKCKLWY

Euphagus cyanocephalus

BLACKBIRD/COWBIRD SUBFAMILY

Although Brewer's and rusty blackbirds may look similar their choice of habitat is very different. Brewer's prefer shrubby areas near prairies, open meadows, pastures, and human-altered environments such as lawns, golf courses, and parks. Males are black with purplish iridescence on the head and neck and a greenish gloss on the body. The head, neck, and underparts of breeding females are dusty gray with darker and glossier upperparts. Males have whitish eyes while those of the females are dark brown. Both have sharply pointed bills. Females are smaller than the males and turn a somewhat paler buffy gray in autumn plumage. This blackbird is fairly common in the foothills but scarce in the mountains throughout the Canadian Rockies. They nest on the ground, in bushes, or in trees, sometimes in loose colonies.

Brown-headed Cowbird (13 cm)

BJKCKLWY

Molothrus ater

BLACKBIRD/COWBIRD SUBFAMILY

The brown-headed cowbird never builds a nest and does not incubate and care for its young. During the absence of the rightful owners, a female cowbird will slip in, lay one of its eggs in the unguarded nest, often eating or removing one of the host's eggs to keep the number the same, and then take off. Usually the host species will accept the foreign egg without protest, but at other times the offending egg will be covered with a new nest lining or the nest totally deserted. Once the foster parents accept the foreign egg they do not make any distinction between it and their own. The young cowbird often hatches early so it is strong and well grown before the proper occupants are incubated. Because of greater size and strength, it may monopolize the foster parents' ceaseless efforts to feed the brood and the rightful young often perish. Adult males have a brown head and neck and a glossy black body. Females are a brownish gray, darker above. Both sexes have short, conical, sparrowlike bills and short tails. Brown-headed cowbirds are common around foothill ranches, campgrounds, and towns throughout our area.

Rusty Blackbird

Brewer's Blackbird

Brown-headed Cowbird (male and female)

145

Rosy Finch (15 cm)

BJKCKWY

Leucosticte arctoa

FINCH FAMILY

Rosy finches, along with white-tailed ptarmigan, horned larks, and water pipits, are characteristic birds of the alpine region. Uniquely adapted to alpine environments, rosy finches have long, pointed wings for coping with strong winds at high elevations and a pair of pockets on the bottom of the mouth, which develop during the nesting season, that apparently allow the parents to carry large quantities of food to the young. This sparrow-sized, chocolate brown bird has a black crown bordered by a broad gray band over most of the side of the head and neck with a rosy pink wash on the wings and rump. Females are slightly duller and paler. Plumage of either sex can be variable, depending on the subspecies. Rosy finches are usually seen at the edge of retreating snow, eating seeds and berries of tundra plants, spiders, and insects. In particular, they congregate on snowbanks and feed on snow worms. After autumn storms these finches gather into flocks and move to lower valleys and foothills, where they feed on weeds and grain, and at livestock-feeding areas. Later in the year they move farther east and west, returning to the foothills and lower valleys by February. Nesting in crevices of cliffs or under rocks on mountain summits, the rosy finch is a common breeding bird from Waterton to north of Jasper.

Pine Grosbeak (20 cm)

BJKCKLWY

Pinicola enucleator

FINCH FAMILY

A large and handsome finch, the pine grosbeak is a hardy species with an attractive plumage and a pleasing song. Adult males have brilliant rosy red plumage with contrasting gray sides and belly. Females and immatures are grayish overall with a dull yellowish-tinged head and rump. Both sexes display distinct white wing bars and have dark, stubby, curved bills. The powerful bill is used to extract seeds from cones of pine and spruce. They also use the seeds of birch, alder, and Manitoba maple; the fruits of mountain ash, snowberries, roses, and crabapples; and sunflower seeds from feeders as ready sources of nourishment. When flying the pine grosbeak has a deep, undulating flight pattern. They are fairly common in coniferous forests in the subalpine zone throughout the Canadian Rockies, nesting in low conifer branches along the edge of a stand. Pine grosbeaks are not migratory, but they move to lower elevations during the winter where they are seen in small flocks.

Rosy Finch

Pine Grosbeak (male)

Pine Grosbeak (female)

147

Purple Finch (14 cm)
Carpodacus purpureus

BJKCKLWY
FINCH FAMILY

Like the male pine grosbeak, the adult male purple finch is a rose red over the head, breast, upper belly, flanks, and rump, but it is sparrow-sized rather than robin-sized. The back is rose red with streaks and the lower belly and undertail coverts are whitish and unstreaked. Males do not acquire their brilliant plumage until the second year. Females have dark brown upperparts with streaks and whitish buff underparts with conspicuous dark brown streaks, except for the undertail coverts which are unmarked. In addition, females have a distinctive face pattern including dark brown cheeks and mustache outlined with a whitish eyebrow. The notched tails of both sexes are brownish and unmarked. This finch is one of the finest songsters in the Rockies. His song, consisting of exquisite whistles and soft chirps, is complex and energetic. Although preferring conifers for nesting, purple finches generally feed in deciduous trees. Thus open, mixed forests are preferred for nesting, as are townsites. These finches are migrants in the south and occasional breeding birds from Kananaskis northward throughout the Rockies.

Red Crossbill (14 cm)
Loxia curvirostra

BJKCKWY
FINCH FAMILY

The unique crossing tips of the bills of the crossbill are used for extracting seeds from the cones of conifers. This is accomplished by inserting the closed bills into the side of a cone and then opening them. This action husks off the scales, leaving the seeds exposed. While feeding, red crossbills use their bills and feet like parrots, often hanging upside-down. These sparrow-sized birds have a big head and short tail. The male is brick red, brightest on the crown and rump, with a black tail and wings. Adult females have grayish olive plumage with a greenish yellow rump and sometimes greenish yellow streaking on the breast and back. Both sexes lack wing bars. There is a legend that as Jesus suffered on the cross, a bird attempted to pull the nails from His hands and feet. In doing so the bird's bill became badly twisted and its feathers covered in blood. That small bird, so the legend concluded, was a crossbill. Red crossbills, usually in small flocks, are fairly common year-round residents in lodgepole-pine forests throughout our area, generally nesting well out on a conifer branch.

Purple Finch (male)

Purple Finch (female)

Red Crossbill

White-winged Crossbill (15 cm)

BJKCKLWY

Loxia leucoptera

FINCH FAMILY

Although a good field mark only at close range, the crossed mandibles identify both crossbill species. Black wings with white-tipped tertials and two bold white wing bars separate the white-winged from the red crossbill. The male white-winged is a rosier red than the red crossbill, but there is a considerable variation in tint and shade. Noticeably smaller than the look-alike male pine grosbeak, the white-winged crossbill has more prominent wing bars and its smaller bill is crossed at the tip. Females are a grayish olive with dark streaks, similar to the female red crossbill except for the wing bars. These gregarious birds are closely associated with coniferous forests or mixed forests where spruce predominate. They feed largely upon the seeds of spruce and fir, rather than pine as preferred by the red crossbill. Their highly irregular wanderings are dependent upon cone crops. They may be present in an area for a few years and then totally absent the next. White-winged crossbills are common year-round residents of the Canadian Rockies.

✓Common Redpoll (13 cm)

BJKCKLWY

Carduelis flammea

FINCH FAMILY

The hardy little common redpoll winters throughout most of the Canadian Rockies from November through April. Common redpolls can be recognized by their red cap and blackish chin. In addition, the breast and cheeks of the adult males are pink, with the pink often spreading onto the flanks and rump. Both sexes have buffy upperparts heavily streaked with gray and white especially on the rump, and white underparts with dusky streaks mainly on the sides and undertail coverts. These common winter visitors form flocks of various sizes. Upon close examination of flocks of these unwary birds, you may note some that are whiter than the rest with white rumps and generally no streaks on the undertail coverts. The males have a delicate pink blush on their breasts. These may be hoary redpolls *(Carduelis hornemanni)* that often associate with the common. The variation in plumage of these two birds is so great that it can be impossible to distinguish them in the field.

✓Pine Siskin (11 cm)

BJKCKLWY

Carduelis pinus

FINCH FAMILY

Pine siskins are small, dark finches that are very sociable, noisy, and generally found in small flocks. Although the plumage is variable, they are usually heavily and uniformly streaked with grayish brown. The bases of the wing and tail feathers are yellow, forming diagnostic yellow patches that are most noticeable when the bird is in flight. Two whitish or buffy bars are present on the wings. Their underparts are white with dusky streaks except on the abdomen. They have narrow, pointed bills. Although pine siskins are associated with conifers, they generally feed on the seeds of birches, alders, and conifers. These unwary siskins can be attracted to feeders as well. They have a hoarse, canarylike song and several calls. Pine siskins are a common breeding bird in the montane zone throughout our area, usually nesting in a conifer. These birds may stay in the Rockies until December.

White-winged Crossbill

Common Redpoll

Pine Siskin

Evening Grosbeak (18 cm)

Coccothraustes vespertinus

BJKCKLWY

FINCH FAMILY

The evening grosbeak is a plump, sturdy finch about cowbird-size. It is a handsome bird with richly colored plumage and a powerful bill. The plumage of the adult male is spectacular, with golden body feathers and a prominent gold band across the forehead while the rest of the head, upper back, and breast are a rich brown. The comparatively subdued females are silver-gray in appearance, tinted below with yellow. Both sexes have black wings with distinct white patches. Males have black tails and females have black tails with white spots near the end. Their long, cone-shaped bills are bone colored during the winter, but they undergo a change in pigmentation to greenish yellow by early spring. Evening grosbeaks are primarily seed eaters. During the breeding season they feed on conifer seeds and wild berries. During the winter flocks of these gregarious birds descend to lower elevations to feed on seed-bearing trees such as Manitoba maple and green ash that are covered with winged seeds. The powerful, overlapping mandibles are used to expose the soft nut within. Evening grosbeaks are readily lured to sunflower seed feeders, where they brighten up even the bleakest winter day. They are also attracted to salt and fine gravel along roads. Evening grosbeaks are noisy with a wide repertoire of calls and cries. They are year-round residents in all but the extreme northern portion of our area. During the breeding season they are fairly common in the subalpine zone of the eastern slopes and scarce on the western slopes.

House Sparrow (13 cm)

Passer domesticus

BJKCKLWY

OLD-WORLD SPARROW FAMILY

The house sparrow is probably the first bird most people learn to recognize. It was introduced to New York from Europe in 1850 and it is now omnipresent in almost all populated areas on the continent except the north. This adaptable little bird is not a sparrow at all, but a weaver finch. In breeding plumage, the male has a gray crown, black throat and upper breast, whitish cheeks, chestnut nape, streaked back, a single bold white wing bar, a small white spot behind the eye, and a black bill. In winter, the bill is a brownish yellow and the black plumage is confined to the chin. Much plainer adult females and juveniles have brownish gray upperparts, streaked with black and buff on the back and wings, with a buffy facial line that hooks down behind the eye and goes over the ear. House sparrows have a monotonous *"chirp"* or *"chisseck"* call that is repeated over and over. Full of energy, they are extremely boisterous and pugnacious. They nest in buildings, bird boxes, swallow nests, natural cavities, woodpecker holes, and in domed structures that they build in tree branches. Gregarious by nature, house sparrows are very common year-round residents in towns and other human settlements in the montane zone throughout the Canadian Rockies.

Evening Grosbeak (male)

Evening Grosbeak (female)

House Sparrow

Glossary

Abdomen That part of the under surface of the body between the breast and the undertail coverts.

Accidental A species that appeared in a given area a few times only and whose normal range is in another region.

Adult A bird that has assumed its final or definitive plumage type, in contrast to immature plumage of subadult, immature, or juvenile.

Axillars A group of feathers, usually elongated, at the armpit between the wing and the body.

Back The portion of the upperparts located behind the nape and between the wings.

Barred Having stripes across the feathers.

Belly The portion of the underparts between the breast and the undertail coverts.

Belted Having a band across breast or belly.

Bib An area of contrasting color on the chin, throat, upper breast, or all of these.

Breast The area of the underparts between the foreneck and the belly.

Breast band A band of contrasting color that runs across the breast.

Breeding plumage A coat of feathers worn by an adult bird during the breeding season.

Breeding range The geographic area in which a species nests.

Call A brief vocalization with a relatively simple acoustical structure, usually given year-round by both sexes.

Cap An area of contrasting color on the top of the head.

Carrion Dead and decaying flesh.

Cheek The side of the face.

Chin The area immediately below the base of the lower mandible.

Clutch A group of eggs laid by one bird.

Collar A band of contrasting color that runs across the foreneck, hindneck, or both.

Colonial Nesting in groups or colonies.

Comb A thick, usually red, fleshy piece on the top of the head of some birds.

Coniferous Trees that bear cones.

Coverts Small feathers that cover the bases of other, usually larger, feathers.

Crest A tuft of elongated feathers on top of the head.

Crown Top of the head.

Dabbling To feed by kicking in the water so head reaches for the bottom as rear end points upward.

Deciduous Trees which shed leaves annually.

Decurved Down-curved.

Dimorphic Existing in two different forms or colors.

Ear tuft A group of elongated feathers above the eyes that resemble ears.

Eclipse plumage A dull-colored coat of feathers acquired by some male ducks and a few other birds immediately after mating.

Eyebrow A stripe on the side of the head immediately above the eye.

Eyeline A straight, thin, horizontal stripe on the side of the face, running through the eye.

Eye-ring A fleshy or feathered ring around the eye, often distinctively colored.

Facial disk The feathers that encircle the eyes of some birds.

Family A taxonomic group composed of related genera.

Field mark A characteristic of color, pattern, or structure useful in identifying a species in the field.

Flank The rear portion of the side of a bird's body.

Gorget A covering of brilliant feathers on the throat of male hummingbirds.

Gregarious Spending much of the time in flocks.

Hawking To fly at or attack on the wing.

Hood A distinctively colored area usually covering most or all of the head.

Immature A bird that has not yet begun to breed, and often has not acquired adult plumage.

Indigenous Originating in the region where found.

Insectivorous Insect-eating.

Introduced Established by humans in an area outside the natural range.

Iridescence A display of lustrous colors.

Iris The colored part of the eye surrounding the black pupil.

Lore The area between the eye and the base of the upper mandible.

Mandibles The two halves of a bird's bill.

Mantle The plumage of the back and upper surface of the wings.

Median crown stripe A stripe of contrasting color along the center of the crown.

Migrant A bird in the process of migrating between its breeding area and its winter range.

Migration A regular, periodic movement between two regions, generally a breeding area and a wintering area.

Mixedwood Composed of both coniferous and deciduous trees.

Mustache (Malar stripe) A colored streak of feathers running back from the base of the bill.

Nail A horny tip of the upper mandible of some waterfowl.

Nape The back of the neck.

Necklace A band of spots or streaks across the breast or around the neck.

Nocturnal Active in the night.

Omnivorous Eating any kind of animal and vegetable matter.

Ornithology The scientific study of birds.

Peeps A collective name applied to the smallest species of sandpipers. Although not a systematic group, they are similar enough in habit and general appearance to be popularly grouped together.

Permanent resident A bird that remains in one area throughout the year.

Plumage The feathers of a bird.

Primaries The outermost and longest flight feathers of the wing.

Raptors Birds of prey such as hawks and eagles.

Rump The back portion of a bird at the base of the tail feathers.

Scapulars A group of feathers on the shoulder of a bird along the side of the back.

Secondaries Flight feathers attached to the forearm of the wing.

Side The lateral part of the breast and belly.

Song A specific and often complex pattern of notes, usually given only by the male during the breeding season for defending a breeding territory and attracting a mate.

Speculum A patch on the wing of ducks, usually rectangular, contrasting in color with the rest of the wing and often brightly colored and more or less iridescent.

Stray A bird found outside of its normal range.

Streaked Having a pattern of vertical or longitudinal stripes.

Stripe Elongated marking running lengthwise of the bird.

Subadult A bird that has not yet acquired adult plumage.

Summer resident A bird that remains in an area during the summer but winters elsewhere.

Talons Long, sharp, curved claws of a bird of prey.

Terrestrial Frequenting the ground.

Thermals Rising currents of natural hot air used by soaring birds.

Throat The area of the underparts between the chin and the breast.

Trailing edge The posterior edge of the extended wing, consisting of the tips of the primaries and secondaries.

Transient A bird that occurs at a location only during migration between the winter and breeding ranges.

Underparts The lower surface of the body, including the chin, throat, breast, belly, sides, flanks, and undertail coverts.

Undertail coverts The small feathers that lie beneath and cover the base of the tail feathers.

Upperparts The upper surface of the body, including the crown, nape, back, scapulars, rump, and uppertail coverts.

Vagrant A bird occurring outside of its normal range.

Web A fleshy membrane that unites the toes of some water birds.

Wing bar A stripe or bar of contrasting color on the upper surface of the wing, formed by the tips of one of the rows of wing coverts.

Wing coverts Small feathers that overlie and cover the base of the large flight feathers.

Winter plumage The feathers worn by a bird during the nonbreeding season.

Wrist The forward-projecting angle or bend of the wing.

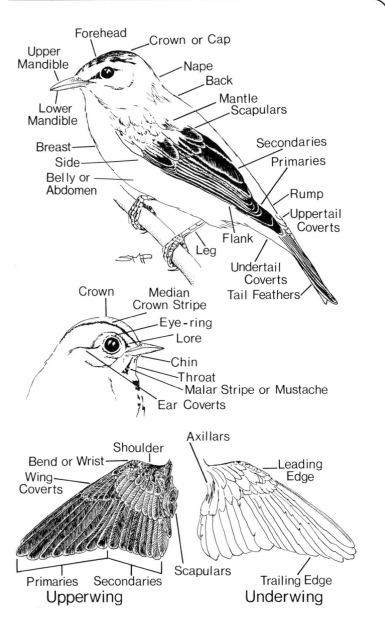

Figure 4. Parts of a bird.

Checklist

This is a list of all birds recorded for the Canadian Rocky Mountains. Readers may wish to use this list to record the species they have seen.

		B¹	J	KC	K	L	W	Y
[ ] Red-throated Loon	*Gavia stellata*	P	P	H		P	P	
[ ] Arctic Loon	*Gavia arctica*							P
[ ] Pacific Loon	*Gavia pacifica*	P	P			B	P	
[ ] Common Loon	*Gavia immer*	B	B	B	P	B	P	P
[ ] Yellow-billed Loon	*Gavia adamsii*			H				
[ ] Pied-billed Grebe	*Podilymbus podiceps*	B	P	B	P	P	B	
[ ] Horned Grebe	*Podiceps auritus*	P	P	P	P	B	P	P
[ ] Red-necked Grebe	*Podiceps grisegena*	B	B	B	P	B	B	P
[ ] Eared Grebe	*Podiceps nigricollis*	P	P	P	P	P	P	P
[ ] Western Grebe	*Aechmophorus occidentalis*	P	P	P	P	P	P	P
[ ] Clark's Grebe	*Aechmophorus clarkii*			H			H	
[ ] American White Pelican	*Pelecanus erythrorhynchos*	P	P				P	
[ ] Double-crested Cormorant	*Phalacrocorax auritus*		P			P	P	
[ ] American Bittern	*Botaurus lentiginosus*	B	P	P			P	P
[ ] Great Blue Heron	*Ardea herodias*	P	P	P	P	P	P	B
[ ] Great Egret	*Casmerodius albus*	P						
[ ] Green-backed Heron	*Butorides striatus*	P						
[ ] Fulvous Whistling-Duck	*Dendrocygna bicolor*						H	
[ ] Tundra Swan	*Cygnus columbianus*	P	P	P	P	P	P	P
[ ] Trumpeter Swan	*Cygnus buccinator*	P	P	P	P	B	P	P
[ ] Greater White-fronted Goose	*Anser albifrons*			P		P		
[ ] Snow Goose	*Chen caerulescens*	P	P	P	P	P	P	P
[ ] Brant	*Branta bernicla*		P					
[ ] Canada Goose	*Branta canadensis*	B	B	B	B	B	B	B
[ ] Wood Duck	*Aix sponsa*	B	B			B	P	
[ ] Green-winged Teal	*Anas crecca*	B	B	B	B	P	P	B
[ ] Mallard	*Anas platyrhynchos*	B	B	B	B	P	B	B
[ ] Northern Pintail	*Anas acuta*	P	P	P	P	P	P	P
[ ] Blue-winged Teal	*Anas discors*	B	B	B	B	P	B	P
[ ] Cinnamon Teal	*Anas cyanoptera*	B	P	P	P		P	P
[ ] Northern Shoveler	*Anas clypeata*	P	P	P	P	P	P	P
[ ] Gadwall	*Anas strepera*	P	P	P			P	P
[ ] Eurasian Wigeon	*Anas penelope*		P				P	
[ ] American Wigeon	*Anas americana*	B	P	P	B	P	P	P
[ ] Canvasback	*Aythya valisineria*	P	P	P		P	P	P
[ ] Redhead	*Aythya americana*	P	P	P	P	P	P	P

B¹ = Banff National Park, J = Jasper National Park, KC = Kananaskis Country, K = Kootenay National Park, L = Liard River Hotsprings and the northern Canadian Rockies, W = Waterton Lakes National Park, Y = Yoho National Park.

B = Species known to have bred in the area, P = Species known to have occurred in the area, H = A questionable record that needs verification.

			B¹	J	KC	K	L	W	Y
[ ]	Ring-necked Duck	*Aythya collaris*	B	B	B	B	B	B	B
[ ]	Greater Scaup	*Aythya marila*		P				P	
[ ]	Lesser Scaup	*Aythya affinis*	B	B	B	P	B	P	P
[ ]	Harlequin Duck	*Histrionicus histrionicus*	B	B	B	B		B	B
[ ]	Oldsquaw	*Clangula hyemalis*	P	P	P		P	P	
[ ]	Surf Scoter	*Melanitta perspicillata*	P	P	P	P	P	P	P
[ ]	White-winged Scoter	*Melanitta fusca*	P	P	P	P	P	P	P
[ ]	Common Goldeneye	*Bucephala clangula*	P	P	B	P	P	B	P
[ ]	Barrow's Goldeneye	*Bucephala islandica*	B	B	B	P	P	B	B
[ ]	Bufflehead	*Bucephala albeola*	P	P	P	B	B	B	P
[ ]	Hooded Merganser	*Lophodytes cucullatus*	P	P	P	P		B	P
[ ]	Common Merganser	*Mergus merganser*	B	B	B	B	P	B	B
[ ]	Red-breasted Merganser	*Mergus serrator*	P	P	P	P	P	P	P
[ ]	Ruddy Duck	*Oxyura jamaicensis*	P	P	P	P	P	P	P
[ ]	Turkey Vulture	*Cathartes aura*	P		P			P	
[ ]	Osprey	*Pandion haliaetus*	B	B	B	P	P	B	B
[ ]	Bald Eagle	*Haliaeetus leucocephalus*	B	B	B	P	B	B	B
[ ]	Northern Harrier	*Circus cyaneus*	P	P	P	P	P	B	P
[ ]	Sharp-shinned Hawk	*Accipiter striatus*	B	P	B	P	B	B	P
[ ]	Cooper's Hawk	*Accipiter cooperii*	B	B	B	B		B	B
[ ]	Northern Goshawk	*Accipiter gentilis*	B	B	B	P	B	B	P
[ ]	Broad-winged Hawk	*Buteo platypterus*	P		P			P	
[ ]	Swainson's Hawk	*Buteo swainsoni*	P	P	P	P		P	P
[ ]	Red-tailed Hawk	*Buteo jamaicensis*	B	B	B	B	P	B	B
[ ]	Ferruginous Hawk	*Buteo regalis*	P	P	P			P	P
[ ]	Rough-legged Hawk	*Buteo lagopus*	P	P	P	P	P	P	P
[ ]	Golden Eagle	*Aquila chrysaetos*	B	B	B	B	P	B	B
[ ]	American Kestrel	*Falco sparverius*	B	B	B	B	P	B	B
[ ]	Merlin	*Falco columbarius*	B	P	P	P	P	P	B
[ ]	Peregrine Falcon	*Falco peregrinus*	P	P	B		P	P	H
[ ]	Gyrfalcon	*Falco rusticolus*	P	P	P			H	
[ ]	Prairie Falcon	*Falco mexicanus*	P	P	B	H		P	
[ ]	Gray Partridge	*Perdix perdix*	P	P	P			P	
[ ]	Ring-necked Pheasant	*Phasianus colchicus*	P					P	
[ ]	Spruce Grouse	*Dendragapus canadensis*	B	B	B	B	P	B	B
[ ]	Blue Grouse	*Dendragapus obscurus*	B	B	B	B	P	B	B
[ ]	Willow Ptarmigan	*Lagopus lagopus*		B					
[ ]	White-tailed Ptarmigan	*Lagopus leucurus*	B	B	B	B	B	B	B
[ ]	Ruffed Grouse	*Bonasa umbellus*	B	B	B	B	B	B	B
[ ]	Greater Prairie-Chicken	*Tympanuchus cupido*						H	
[ ]	Sharp-tailed Grouse	*Tympanuchus phasianellus*	P	P			B	B	B
[ ]	Yellow Rail	*Coturnicops noveboracensis*		P					
[ ]	Virginia Rail	*Rallus limicola*	P						
[ ]	Sora	*Porzana carolina*	B	B	B	P	P	P	P
[ ]	American Coot	*Fulica americana*	P	P	B	B	P	P	P
[ ]	Sandhill Crane	*Grus canadensis*			P	P		P	
[ ]	Whooping Crane	*Grus americana*						H	
[ ]	Black-bellied Plover	*Pluvialis squatarola*	P	P				P	P

159

			B¹	J	KC	K	L	W	Y
[ ]	Lesser Golden-Plover	*Pluvialis dominica*	P	P			P		P
[ ]	Semipalmated Plover	*Charadrius semipalmatus*	P	P	P		P	H	P
[ ]	Killdeer	*Charadrius vociferus*	B	B	B	B	B	B	B
[ ]	American Avocet	*Recurvirostra americana*	P					P	P
[ ]	Greater Yellowlegs	*Tringa melanoleuca*	P	B	B	H	P	P	
[ ]	Lesser Yellowlegs	*Tringa flavipes*	P	P	P	P	P	P	P
[ ]	Solitary Sandpiper	*Tringa solitaria*	B	B	B	B	P	P	B
[ ]	Wandering Tattler	*Heteroscelus incanus*		P				P	
[ ]	Spotted Sandpiper	*Actitis macularia*	B	B	B	B	B	B	B
[ ]	Upland Sandpiper	*Bartramia longicauda*	P	P	P		P	B	P
[ ]	Eskimo Curlew	*Numenius borealis*		H					
[ ]	Long-billed Curlew	*Numenius americanus*	P					P	
[ ]	Hudsonian Godwit	*Limosa haemastica*					P		P
[ ]	Marbled Godwit	*Limosa fedoa*		H	P			P	
[ ]	Ruddy Turnstone	*Arenaria interpres*	P						
[ ]	Sanderling	*Calidris alba*	P	P	P			P	
[ ]	Semipalmated Sandpiper	*Calidris pusilla*	P	P			P	H	P
[ ]	Western Sandpiper	*Calidris mauri*		P		H	P		P
[ ]	Least Sandpiper	*Calidris minutilla*	P	P	P	P	P	H	P
[ ]	Baird's Sandpiper	*Calidris bairdii*	P	P	P	P	P	H	P
[ ]	Pectoral Sandpiper	*Calidris melanotos*	P	P	P		P	P	P
[ ]	Dunlin	*Calidris alpina*		P					
[ ]	Stilt Sandpiper	*Calidris himantopus*		P					P
[ ]	Buff-breasted Sandpiper	*Tryngites subruficollis*		P					
[ ]	Short-billed Dowitcher	*Limnodromus griseus*	P			H		P	P
[ ]	Long-billed Dowitcher	*Limnodromus scolopaceus*	P	P			P		H
[ ]	Common Snipe	*Gallinago gallinago*	B	B	B	P	B	P	B
[ ]	Wilson's Phalarope	*Phalaropus tricolor*	P	P	P	P	H	P	P
[ ]	Red-necked Phalarope	*Phalaropus lobatus*	P	P	P	P	P	H	P
[ ]	Red Phalarope	*Phalaropus fulicaria*	P						
[ ]	Parasitic Jaeger	*Stercorarius parasiticus*	P	P	P		H	P	
[ ]	Long-tailed Jaeger	*Stercorarius longicaudus*	P	P	P	P			P
[ ]	Franklin's Gull	*Larus pipixcan*	P	P	P			P	
[ ]	Bonaparte's Gull	*Larus philadelphia*	P	P	P	P	P	P	P
[ ]	Mew Gull	*Larus canus*	P	P			B		P
[ ]	Ring-billed Gull	*Larus delawarensis*	P	P	P	P		P	P
[ ]	California Gull	*Larus californicus*	P	P	P	P		P	P
[ ]	Herring Gull	*Larus argentatus*	P	P	P		B	H	P
[ ]	Thayer's Gull	*Larus thayeri*		P	H				
[ ]	Black-legged Kittiwake	*Rissa tridactyla*		P					
[ ]	Sabine's Gull	*Xema sabini*	P	P	P	P		P	
[ ]	Caspian Tern	*Sterna caspia*	P		P				
[ ]	Common Tern	*Sterna hirundo*	P	P	P				P
[ ]	Forster's Tern	*Sterna forsteri*	P	P				P	
[ ]	Black Tern	*Chlidonias niger*	P	P	P			P	P
[ ]	Rock Dove	*Columba livia*	P	P	P	P		P	P
[ ]	Band-tailed Pigeon	*Columba fasciata*	P	P	P			P	
[ ]	Mourning Dove	*Zenaida macroura*	P	B	B	P	P	P	P

				B[1]	J	KC	K	L	W	Y
[ ]	Black-billed Cuckoo	*Coccyzus erythropthalmus*							P	
[ ]	Flammulated Owl	*Otus flammeolus*					H		H	
[ ]	Western Screech-Owl	*Otus kennicottii*	P			P		P	
[X]	Great Horned Owl	*Bubo virginianus*	B	B	B	B	B	B	P
[ ]	Snowy Owl	*Nyctea scandiaca*	P	P			P		
[ ]	Northern Hawk-Owl	*Surnia ulula*	B	P	B	B	B		B
[ ]	Northern Pygmy-Owl	*Glaucidium gnoma*	B	P	P	P		P	P
[ ]	Burrowing Owl	*Athene cunicularia*	P	P					
[ ]	Barred Owl	*Strix varia*	B	B	B	B	P	P	B
[ ]	Great Gray Owl	*Strix nebulosa*	P	P	P	B	P	P	P
[ ]	Long-eared Owl	*Asio otus*	B						P
[ ]	Short-eared Owl	*Asio flammeus*	P	P	P	P	P	P	P
[ ]	Boreal Owl	*Aegolius funereus*	P	B	B	P	P		P
[ ]	Northern Saw-whet Owl	*Aegolius acadicus*	B	P	B	P		P	
[ ]	Common Nighthawk	*Chordeiles minor*	B	P	B	B	B	P	P
[ ]	Common Poorwill	*Phalaenoptilus nuttallii*			P	P			H
[ ]	Black Swift	*Cypseloides niger*	B	B	P	P		P	P
[ ]	Vaux's Swift	*Chaetura vauxi*			H	P		P	P
[ ]	White-throated Swift	*Aeronautes saxatalis*						H	
[ ]	Ruby-throated Hummingbird	*Archilochus colubris*		P				P	
[ ]	Black-chinned Hummingbird	*Archilochus alexandri*					H		
[ ]	Anna's Hummingbird	*Calypte anna*						P	P
[ ]	Calliope Hummingbird	*Stellula calliope*	P	P	B	B		B	P
[ ]	Rufous Hummingbird	*Selasphorus rufus*	B	B	B	P	P	B	B
[ ]	Belted Kingfisher	*Ceryle alcyon*	B	P	B	B	B	B	B
[ ]	Lewis' Woodpecker	*Melanerpes lewis*	P	B	P			B	
[ ]	Red-headed Woodpecker	*Melanerpes erythrocephalus*	P		P			P	
[ ]	Yellow-bellied Sapsucker	*Sphyrapicus varius*	B	B	B	B	B	P	B
[ ]	Red-naped Sapsucker	*Sphyrapicus nuchalis*	B	B	B	B		B	B
[ ]	Red-breasted Sapsucker	*Sphyrapicus ruber*					P		
[ ]	Williamson's Sapsucker	*Sphyrapicus thyroideus*						P	H
[ ]	Downy Woodpecker	*Picoides pubescens*	B	P	B	P	P	B	B
[ ]	Hairy Woodpecker	*Picoides villosus*	B	B	B	B	P	B	B
[ ]	Three-toed Woodpecker	*Picoides tridactylus*	B	B	B	B	P	B	B
[ ]	Black-backed Woodpecker	*Picoides arcticus*	P	P	P	B	P	B	P
[ ]	Northern Flicker	*Colaptes auratus*	B	B	B	B	B	B	B
[ ]	Pileated Woodpecker	*Dryocopus pileatus*	B	B	B	B	P	B	B
[ ]	Olive-sided Flycatcher	*Contopus borealis*	P	B	B	P	P	P	B
[ ]	Western Wood-Pewee	*Contopus sordidulus*	P	P	B	B		B	B
[ ]	Yellow-bellied Flycatcher	*Empidonax flaviventris*	P		P				
[ ]	Alder Flycatcher	*Empidonax alnorum*	P	P	B	P	P	P	P
[ ]	Willow Flycatcher	*Empidonax traillii*	P	P	B	P		P	B
[ ]	Least Flycatcher	*Empidonax minimus*	B	P	B	P		P	P
[ ]	Hammond's Flycatcher	*Empidonax hammondii*	P	P	B	B		B	P
[ ]	Dusky Flycatcher	*Empidonax oberholseri*	B	B	B	B		B	P
[ ]	Western Flycatcher	*Empidonax difficilis*	B	P	B	B		P	P
[ ]	Eastern Phoebe	*Sayornis phoebe*	P	P	B		H	H	P

		B¹	J	KC	K	L	W	Y
[ ] Say's Phoebe	*Sayornis saya*	P	P	B			P	P	P
[ ] Vermilion Flycatcher	*Pyrocephalus rubinus*					H		
[ ] Western Kingbird	*Tyrannus verticalis*	P	P	P	P		P	
[ ] Eastern Kingbird	*Tyrannus tyrannus*	B	P	B	B		B	P
[ ] Scissor-tailed Flycatcher	*Tyrannus forficatus*					H		
[ ] Horned Lark	*Eremophila alpestris*	B	B	B	P	H	P	P
[ ] Purple Martin	*Progne subis*					H		
[ ] Tree Swallow	*Tachycineta bicolor*	B	B	B	B	P	B	B
[ ] Violet-green Swallow	*Tachycineta thalassina*	B	B	B	B	P	B	B
[ ] Northern Rough-winged Swallow	*Stelgidopteryx serripennis*	B	B	B	B	H	B	B
[ ] Bank Swallow	*Riparia riparia*	P	B	B	B	P	P	P
[ ] Cliff Swallow	*Hirundo pyrrhonota*	B	B	B	B	P	B	B
[ ] Barn Swallow	*Hirundo rustica*	B	B	B	B	P	B	B
⊠ Gray Jay	*Perisoreus canadensis*	B	P	B	B	B	B	B
[ ] Stellar's Jay	*Cyanocitta stelleri*	P	P	P	B	P	B	B
[X] Blue Jay	*Cyanocitta cristata*	P	P	P		P	H	
[ ] Clark's Nutcracker	*Nucifraga columbiana*	B	B	B	B		B	B
[ ] Black-billed Magpie	*Pica pica*	B	B	B	P	P	B	B
[ ] American Crow	*Corvus brachyrhynchos*	B	B	B	P	B	B	B
[ ] Common Raven	*Corvus corax*	B	B	B	B	P	B	B
[X] Black-capped Chickadee	*Parus atricapillus*	B	B	B	B	P	B	B
[X] Mountain Chickadee	*Parus gambeli*	B	B	B	B		P	B
[X] Boreal Chickadee	*Parus hudsonicus*	P	B	B	B	P	P	B
[ ] Chestnut-backed Chickadee	*Parus rufescens*	P		H			P	H
⊠ Red-breasted Nuthatch	*Sitta canadensis*	B	B	B	B	P	B	B
[★] White-breasted Nuthatch	*Sitta carolinensis*	P		P	P		P	P
[ ] Pygmy Nuthatch	*Sitta pygmaea*	P	P					
[ ] Brown Creeper	*Certhia americana*	P	B	P	B		B	B
[ ] Rock Wren	*Salpinctes obsoletus*	P	P	P	P		P	
[ ] House Wren	*Troglodytes aedon*	P	P	B			B	
[ ] Winter Wren	*Troglodytes troglodytes*	B	P	B	B		B	B
[ ] Marsh Wren	*Cistothorus palustris*	P	P	P			P	
[ ] American Dipper	*Cinclus mexicanus*	B	B	B	B	P	B	B
[ ] Golden-crowned Kinglet	*Regulus satrapa*	B	P	B	B	P	P	B
[ ] Ruby-crowned Kinglet	*Regulus calendula*	B	B	B	B	P	B	P
[ ] Eastern Bluebird	*Sialia sialis*	P						
[ ] Western Bluebird	*Sialia mexicana*	P						
[ ] Mountain Bluebird	*Sialia currucoides*	B	B	B	B	B	B	B
[ ] Townsend's Solitaire	*Myadestes townsendi*	B	B	B	B	B	B	B
[ ] Veery	*Catharus fuscescens*	P		B	H		B	P
[ ] Gray-cheeked Thrush	*Catharus minimus*	P	P	P		P		
[ ] Swainson's Thrush	*Catharus ustulatus*	B	B	B	B	P	B	B
[ ] Hermit Thrush	*Catharus guttatus*	B	B	B	B	P	B	B
[ ] American Robin	*Turdus migratorius*	B	B	B	B	B	B	B
[ ] Varied Thrush	*Ixoreus naevius*	P	B	B	B	B	B	B
[ ] Gray Catbird	*Dumetella carolinensis*	P	P	P			B	P
[ ] Northern Mockingbird	*Mimus polyglottos*	P						H

	Common Name	Scientific Name	B¹	J	KC	K	L	W	Y
[ ]	Brown Thrasher	*Toxostoma rufum*	P	P			P		
[ ]	Bendire's Thrasher	*Toxostoma bendirei*	P						
[ ]	Water Pipit	*Anthus spinoletta*	B	B	B	B	P	P	B
[ ]	Sprague's Pipit	*Anthus spragueii*	P					H	
[X]	Bohemian Waxwing	*Bombycilla garrulus*	P	B	P	B	B	B	P
[ ]	Cedar Waxwing	*Bombycilla cedrorum*	B	P	B	P	P	B	B
[X]	Northern Shrike	*Lanius excubitor*	P	P	P	P	P	P	P
[ ]	Loggerhead Shrike	*Lanius ludovicianus*			P	H	P		
[ ]	European Starling	*Sturnus vulgaris*	B	P	B	B	P	B	B
[ ]	Solitary Vireo	*Vireo solitarius*	P	P	B	B	P	P	P
[ ]	Warbling Vireo	*Vireo gilvus*	B	P	B	B	B	P	B
[ ]	Philadelphia Vireo	*Vireo philadelphicus*	P	P					P
[ ]	Red-eyed Vireo	*Vireo olivaceus*	P	P	B	P	P	P	P
[ ]	Tennessee Warbler	*Vermivora peregrina*	P	P	B	P	P	P	P
[ ]	Orange-crowned Warbler	*Vermivora celata*	P	P	B	P	P	P	B
[ ]	Nashville Warbler	*Vermivora ruficapilla*	P		B			P	H
[ ]	Northern Parula	*Parula americana*			P				
[ ]	Yellow Warbler	*Dendroica petechia*	B	B	B	P	P	B	B
[ ]	Chestnut-sided Warbler	*Dendroica pensylvanica*			P				
[ ]	Magnolia Warbler	*Dendroica magnolia*	P	P	P	P	B		P
[ ]	Cape May Warbler	*Dendroica tigrina*	P	P	P	P			
[ ]	Yellow-rumped Warbler	*Dendroica coronata*	B	B	B	B	P	B	B
[ ]	Black-throated Gray Warbler	*Dendroica nigrescens*	P						
[ ]	Townsend's Warbler	*Dendroica townsendi*	B	P	B	B	P	P	B
[ ]	Black-throated Green Warbler	*Dendroica virens*	P		P			P	
[ ]	Palm Warbler	*Dendroica palmarum*	P	P	P		P		P
[ ]	Bay-breasted Warbler	*Dendroica castanea*	H	P		P	P		P
[ ]	Blackpoll Warbler	*Dendroica striata*	P	P	P	P	B	H	P
[ ]	Black-and-white Warbler	*Mniotilta varia*	P	P	P			P	
[ ]	American Redstart	*Setophaga ruticilla*	P	P	B	P	B	P	P
[ ]	Ovenbird	*Seiurus aurocapillus*		P	B		B	P	
[ ]	Northern Waterthrush	*Seiurus noveboracensis*	P	P	B	P	P	P	P
[ ]	Connecticut Warbler	*Oporornis agilis*			P				
[ ]	Mourning Warbler	*Oporornis philadelphia*			B	P			
[ ]	MacGillivray's Warbler	*Oporornis tolmiei*	P	B	B	B	B	B	B
[ ]	Common Yellowthroat	*Geothlypis trichas*	B	P	B	B	P	P	B
[ ]	Wilson's Warbler	*Wilsonia pusilla*	B	P	B	B	P	B	B
[ ]	Canada Warbler	*Wilsonia canadensis*	P	P	P				
[ ]	Yellow-breasted Chat	*Icteria virens*	P		P				
[ ]	Western Tanager	*Piranga ludoviciana*	B	B	B	B	P	B	B
[ ]	Rose-breasted Grosbeak	*Pheucticus ludovicianus*	P	P	P		B	P	P
[ ]	Black-headed Grosbeak	*Pheucticus melanocephalus*	P	P		P		P	
[ ]	Lazuli Bunting	*Passerina amoena*	P	P	P	P		B	P
[ ]	Indigo Bunting	*Passerina cyanea*			B			P	
[ ]	Rufous-sided Towhee	*Pipilo erythrophthalmus*	P	P	P			P	
[ ]	American Tree Sparrow	*Spizella arborea*	P	P	P		P	P	P

		B[1]	J	KC	K	L	W	Y
[ ] Chipping Sparrow	*Spizella passerina*	B	B	B	B	B	B	B
[ ] Clay-colored Sparrow	*Spizella pallida*	P	P	B	P		B	P
[ ] Brewer's Sparrow	*Spizella breweri*	P	B	B	P		B	P
[ ] Vesper Sparrow	*Pooecetes gramineus*	P	P	B	B	P	B	P
[ ] Lark Sparrow	*Chondestes grammacus*							P
[ ] Lark Bunting	*Calamospiza melanocorys*	P			P		B	
[ ] Savannah Sparrow	*Passerculus sandwichensis*	B	B	B	B	P	B	B
[ ] Baird's Sparrow	*Ammodramus bairdii*	P						
[ ] Grasshopper Sparrow	*Ammodramus savannarum*	P					H	
[ ] Le Conte's Sparrow	*Ammodramus leconteii*			P	B	P		B
[ ] Sharp-tailed Sparrow	*Ammodramus caudacutus*	P						
[ ] Fox Sparrow	*Passerella iliaca*	P	B	B	P	P	B	P
[ ] Song Sparrow	*Melospiza melodia*	P	B	B	P	P	B	P
[ ] Lincoln's Sparrow	*Melospiza lincolnii*	B	B	B	B	P	B	P
[ ] Swamp Sparrow	*Melospiza georgiana*	P	P	P		H		
[ ] White-throated Sparrow	*Zonotrichia albicollis*	P	B	B		P	P	
[ ] Golden-crowned Sparrow	*Zonotrichia atricapilla*	B	B	P	P	B		H
[ ] White-crowned Sparrow	*Zonotrichia leucophrys*	B	B	B	B	P	B	B
[ ] Harris' Sparrow	*Zonotrichia querula*	P	P	P			P	P
[✓] Dark-eyed Junco	*Junco hyemalis*	B	B	B	B	B	B	B
[ ] McCown's Longspur	*Calcarius mccownii*						H	
[ ] Lapland Longspur	*Calcarius lapponicus*	P	P	P		H		P
[ ] Smith's Longspur	*Calcarius pictus*						H	
[ ] Chestnut-collared Longspur	*Calcarius ornatus*	P	P				P	
[ ] Snow Bunting	*Plectrophenax nivalis*	P	P	P	P	P	P	P
[ ] Bobolink	*Dolichonyx oryzivorus*	P	P	P		P	B	P
[ ] Red-winged Blackbird	*Agelaius phoeniceus*	B	B	B	B	P	B	B
[ ] Western Meadowlark	*Sturnella neglecta*	P	P	B	P		B	P
[ ] Yellow-headed Blackbird	*Xanthocephalus xanthocephalus*	P	P	P	P	P	B	B
[ ] Rusty Blackbird	*Euphagus carolinus*	P	B	P	P	B		P
[ ] Brewer's Blackbird	*Euphagus cyanocephalus*	B	P	B	P	B	B	B
[ ] Common Grackle	*Quiscalus quiscula*	P	P	P			P	P
[ ] Brown-headed Cowbird	*Molothrus ater*	B	P	B	B	B	B	B
[ ] Northern Oriole	*Icterus galbula*	P	P	B		P	B	P
[ ] Rosy Finch	*Leucosticte arctoa*	B	B	B	B		P	B
[✗] Pine Grosbeak	*Pinicola enucleator*	B	P	B	B	P	P	B
[ ] Purple Finch	*Carpodacus purpureus*	B	B	B	P	P	P	P
[ ] Cassin's Finch	*Carpodacus cassinii*	P	P	B	P		B	P
[ ] House Finch	*Carpodacus mexicanus*		P	P			P	
[ ] Red Crossbill	*Loxia curvirostra*	B	P	B	P		P	P
[ ] White-winged Crossbill	*Loxia leucoptera*	P	P	P	P	P	P	P
[✗] Common Redpoll	*Carduelis flammea*	P	P	P	P	P	P	P
[ ] Hoary Redpoll	*Carduelis hornemanni*	P	P	P		P	P	
[✗] Pine Siskin	*Carduelis pinus*	B	P	B	P	B	B	P
[ ] American Goldfinch	*Carduelis tristis*	P	P	B	P		P	P
[✗] Evening Grosbeak	*Coccothraustes vespertinus*	B	P	P	P	P	P	P
[ ] House Sparrow	*Passer domesticus*	P	P	B	P	P	B	B

164 Rose breasted Grosbeak
American Goldfinch

Selected References

American Ornithologists' Union. 1983. *Check-list of North American Birds.* American Ornithologists' Union. Sixth Edition.

_____. 1985. 35th Supplement to the American Ornithologists' Union Check-list of North American Birds. *Auk* 102:680–86.

Anonymous. 1982. *Kananaskis Country Birds.* Heritage Fund, Government of Alberta, Edmonton, Alberta.

Bellrose, F. C. 1976. *Ducks, Geese and Swans of North America.* Stackpole Books, Harrisburg, Pennsylvania.

Bent, A. C. 1915–1968. *Life Histories of North American Birds.* Dover Publications, New York, New York.

Binford, L. C. 1974. *Birds of Western North America.* MacMillan Publishing Co., New York, New York.

Campbell, R. W., N. K. Dawe, I. McT. Cowan, J. M. Cooper, G. W. Kaiser and M. C. E. McNall. 1989. *The Birds of British Columbia.* Royal British Columbia Museum, Victoria, British Columbia. Volume I. (Volume II on perching birds is scheduled for publication in 1992.)

Clarke, C. H. D., and I. McT. Cowan. 1945. Birds of Banff National Park, Alberta, *Canadian Field-Naturalist* 59:83–103.

Cowan, I. McT. 1955. *Birds of Jasper National Park, Alberta, Canada.* Canadian Wildlife Service, Wildlife Management Bulletin, Ottawa. Series 2, No. 8.

Erskine, A. J. and G. S. Davidson. 1976. Birds in the Fort Nelson Lowlands of Northeastern British Columbia. *Syesis* 9:1–11.

Finlay, J. C. 1984. *A Bird-Finding Guide to Canada.* Hurtig Publishers Ltd., Edmonton, Alberta.

Gadd, B. 1986. *Handbook of the Canadian Rockies.* Corax Press, Jasper, Alberta.

Godfrey, W. E. 1986. *The Birds of Canada.* National Museums of Canada, Ottawa.

Griffith, D. E. 1973. Notes on the Birds at Summit Lake Pass, British Columbia. *Discovery* 2:45–51.

Guiguet, C. J. *The Birds of British Columbia.* British Columbia Provincial Museum Handbook No. 22, Victoria, British Columbia.

Harrison, C. 1984. *A Field Guide to the Nests, Eggs and Nestlings of North American Birds.* Collins, Toronto, Ontario.

Harrison, H. H. 1979. *A Field Guide to Western Birds' Nests.* Houghton Mifflin Co., Boston, Massachusetts.

Holroyd, G. L. and K. J. Van Tighem. 1982. A Birder's Guide to Banff National Park. *Alberta Naturalist* 12:18–24.

_____, eds. 1983. *Ecological (Biophysical) Land Classification of Banff and Jasper National Parks. Vol. 3: The Wildlife Inventory.* Environment Canada, Edmonton, Alberta.

Johnston, W. B. 1949. *An Annotated List of Birds of the East Kootenay, British Columbia.* British Columbia Provincial Museum Occasional Paper No. 7, Victoria, British Columbia.

Kellogg, P. 1975. *A Field Guide to Western Bird Songs.* Houghton Mifflin Co., Boston, Massachusetts. (Three 60-minute cassette tapes).

Munro, J. A. and I. McT. Cowan. 1944. Preliminary Report on the Birds and Mammals of Kootenay National Park, British Columbia. *Canadian Field-Naturalist* 58:34–51.

_____. 1947. *A Review of the Bird Fauna of British Columbia.* British Columbia Provincial Museum, Special Publication 2, Victoria, British Columbia.

National Geographic Society. 1983. *Field Guide to the Birds of North America.* National Geographic Society, Washington, D.C.

Peterson, R. T. 1980. *A Field Guide to Western Birds.* Houghton Mifflin Co., Boston, Massachusetts.

Poll, D. M., M. M. Porter, G. L. Holroyd, R. M. Wershler, and L. W. Gyug. 1984. *Ecological Land Classification of Kootenay National Park, British Columbia. Vol. 2: Wildlife Resource.* Environment Canada, Edmonton, Alberta.

Rand, A. L. 1944. Birds of the Alaska Highway in British Columbia. *Canadian Field-Naturalist* 58:111–25.

_____. 1948. *Birds of Southern Alberta.* National Museum of Canada Bulletin 111, Ottawa.

Robbins, C. S., B. Bruun and H. S. Zim, 1983. *A Guide to Field Identifications, Birds of North America.* Golden Press, New York, New York.

Sadler, T. S. and M. T. Myres. 1976. *Alberta Birds, 1961–1970, with Particular Reference to Migration.* Provincial Museum of Alberta, Natural History Section, Occasional Paper No. 1, Edmonton, Alberta.

Salt, W. R. 1973. *Alberta Vireos and Wood Warblers.* Provincial Museum and Archives of Alberta, Publication 3, Edmonton, Alberta.

Salt, W. R. and A. L. Wilk. 1958. *The Birds of Alberta.* Queen's Printer, Edmonton, Alberta.

Salt, W. R. and J. R. Salt. 1976. *The Birds of Alberta.* Hurtig Publishers, Edmonton, Alberta.

Savage, C. 1985. *The Wonder of Canadian Birds.* Western Producer Prairie Books, Saskatoon, Saskatchewan.

Scoble, R. 1989. *Bird Checklist, Yoho National Park.* Canadian Parks Service, Field, British Columbia.

Scotter, G. W., L. N. Carbyn, W. P. Neily, and J. D. Henry. 1985. *Birds of Nahanni National Park, Northwest Territories.* Saskatchewan Natural History Society Special Publication No. 15, Regina, Saskatchewan.

Sharp, P. L. 1972. *The Birds of Waterton Lakes National Park.* Environment Canada, Edmonton, Alberta.

Udvardy, M. D. F. 1977. *The Audubon Society Field Guide to North American Birds, Western Region.* Random House, Toronto, Ontario.

Ulrich, T. J. 1984. *Birds of the Northern Rockies.* Mountain Press Publishing Company, Missoula, Montana.

Van Tighem, K. and G. Holroyd. 1981. A birder's guide to Jasper National Park. *Alberta Naturalist* 11:134–40.

_____. 1982. *Checklist of the Birds of Banff and Jasper National Parks.* Environment Canada, Edmonton, Alberta.

Van Tighem, K. and A. A. LeMessurier. 1988. *Birding, Jasper National Park.* Parks and People, Jasper, Alberta.

Wade, C. 1977. *The Birds of Yoho National Park.* Report to Parks Canada, Western Region, Calgary, Alberta.

Index of Common Names

Index of Scientific Names

Field Notes

Field Notes

Field Notes

About the Authors

George W. Scotter

Tom J. Ulrich

Edgar T. Jones

George W. Scotter

Born and raised in the shadows of the Rockies in southern Alberta, George Scotter credits frequent family visits to the mountains with stimulating an early interest in nature that developed into a life-long vocation. He has lived and worked in or near the Rockies throughout his life.

With formal training in botany, ecology, taxonomy, and wildlife management, Dr. Scotter has worked in many capacities for the Canadian Wildlife Service of Environment Canada over more than thirty years. At present, he is Chief of Wildlife Conservation based in Edmonton, Alberta and an adjunct professor in Forest Science at the University of Alberta. He has contributed more than 130 articles, mostly on aspects of natural history in western and northern Canada, to major scientific journals and popular magazines, including *Canadian Geographic, Nature Canada*, and *North*. He served as vice-president and later as president of the Canadian Nature Federation, and he is an active member of several other conservation groups. He is the 1985 winner of the prestigious J. B. Harkin medal, awarded for outstanding contributions toward conservation.

Tom J. Ulrich

Born in Chicago, Illinois, Tom Ulrich completed undergraduate and graduate work at Southern Illinois University. During a four-year period of teaching high school biology, he spent his summer vacations traveling through national parks all over the United States and Canada. On one such visit to Glacier National Park, Tom developed a particular admiration and love for mountain goats.

Tom retired from teaching in 1975, purchased a camera outfit, and migrated to Glacier, where he spent several seasons observing and photographing mountain goats. At this time, his career in wildlife photography was launched, and Tom spent extended periods of time in the outdoors capturing numerous bird and mammal species on film. Ulrich's photos have appeared in such publications as *Ranger Rick, National Wildlife, Audubon, American Hunter, Alaska Magazine,* and numerous others. He won the National Wildlife Photo Contest in 1979 and 1981, and in 1987 Tom was named International Wildlife Photographer of the Year for a photograph of a pair of polar bears play-fighting. Tom and his dog, Buddie, live in Montana just outside Glacier National Park. Tom is a frequent visitor to the Canadian Rockies.

Edgar T. Jones

Edgar T. Jones was born in Moose Jaw and moved to Edmonton at age eleven. He trained in natural history with Prof. William Rowan of the University of Alberta and Albert Wolfe, one of the early taxidermists in Edmonton. In 1940 Edgar joined the R.C.A.F. He flew a total of twenty-nine missions as a pilot on Lancaster bombers and was awarded two Distinguished Flying Crosses. After his discharge he formed McMurray Air Services Ltd. out of Ft. McMurray, Alberta. This commercial bush plane operation kept him in the air constantly for the next five years.

In 1950 Edgar moved into the oil business, and in 1951 he formed Alberta Wildlife Tours with Prof. Cy Hampson, another well-known naturalist and nature photographer. Together they pioneered lecturing to thousands of school children on conservation and the wildlife of Alberta. In 1960 his lecturing exploits expanded across North America through the initiation of a seventeen-year relationship with the National Audubon Society out of New York City. In 1961 Edgar formed The Alberta Wildlife Foundation. Recognizing the power of television, Edgar Jones has produced such wildlife series as "Canada Outdoors," "The World Around Us," and "Adventure Outdoors." "Adventure Outdoors" was awarded the Gold Medal for Canada in 1981. He also made presentations of many film productions at the Jubilee Auditorium in Edmonton with such films as *Arctic Canada, Alberta Outdoors, Adventure High Arctic, Fabulous Africa,* and *Kenya Uganda Safari.*

In 1977 the public's expanding interest in wildlife appreciation encouraged him to begin sketching and painting wildlife. His vast photographic collection of "stills" has been used in many books and publications in North America. He lives with his wife, Jeanne, and family in Edmonton.